The Strategy of
Distribution Management

The Marketing Series is one of the most
comprehensive collections of books in marketing
and sales available from the UK today.

Published by Butterworth-Heinemann on behalf of
the Chartered Institute of Marketing, the series is
divided into three distinct groups: *Student* (fulfilling
the needs of those taking the Institute's certificate and
diploma qualifications); *Professional Development*
(for those on formal or self-study vocational training
programmes); and *Practitioner* (presented in a more
informal, motivating and highly practical manner for
the busy marketer).

Formed in 1911, the Chartered Institute of Marketing
is now the largest professional marketing management
body in Europe with over 24,000 members and 28,000
students located worldwide. Its primary objectives are
focused on the development of awareness and
understanding of marketing throughout UK industry
and commerce and on the raising of standards of
professionalism in the education, training and practice
of this key business discipline.

Professional Development Series

The Strategy of Distribution Management

Martin Christopher

Butterworth-Heinemann Ltd
Linacre House, Jordan Hill, Oxford OX2 8DP

A member of the Reed Elsevier plc group

OXFORD   LONDON   BOSTON
MUNICH   NEW DELHI   SINGAPORE   SYDNEY
TOKYO   TORONTO   WELLINGTON

First published 1986
Reprinted 1987, 1989, 1990 (twice), 1991, 1992, 1994

British Library Cataloguing in Publication Data
Christopher, Martin
   The strategy of distribution management
   1. Physical distribution of goods – Management
   I. Title
   658.7'88   HF5415.7

ISBN 0 7506 0367 4

Printed and bound in Great Britain by
Biddles Ltd, Guildford and King's Lynn

Contents

Illustrations

Preface

The importance of logistics management as a means of maintaining and improving corporate profitability has never been greater than it is today. In most developed economies the costs of distribution are steadily growing and account for an increasing proportion of gross national product.

Recession, inflation and technological change have combined to produce an environment in which the options for corporate strategy are much constrained. Yet at the same time for many companies these same conditions have provided a major opportunity for development – specifically, improvements in performance through a revised approach to distribution strategy. This book is about the managerial issues surrounding the creation and implementation of distribution strategies in the wider context of logistics management.

In preparing the manuscript I drew heavily upon the experiences of practising managers with whom I have had the opportunity to work in Europe, North America and Australasia. It is interesting that logistics problems are the same the world over; language, culture, management styles seem not to make the slightest difference to the problems, although often they make a substantial impact upon the solutions.

A similar debt is owed to a large number of colleagues around the world who teach and write about logistics. It is difficult to single out individuals when so much has been learned from so many. However, two colleagues, about as far apart geographically as it is possible to be, have helped my thinking considerably over the years: Professor John Gattorna in Sydney, Australia, and Professor Richard Lancioni in Philadelphia, USA.

Finally, only those who know my bad handwriting will understand my gratitude to the two people who typed and word-processed the various drafts of the manuscripts, Mrs Persephone Knights and Miss Norene Layton.

Martin Christopher
Cranfield

1 The total distribution concept

Logistics has always been a central and essential feature of all economic activity and yet paradoxically it is only in recent years that it has come to receive serious attention from either the business or academic worlds. One obvious reason for this neglect is that whilst the *functions* that comprise the logistics task are individually recognised, the *concept* of logistics as an integrative activity in business has only really developed within the last twenty years.

What is logistics? It can be variously defined, but expressed most simply it is:

> The process of strategically managing the movement and storage of materials, parts, and finished inventory from suppliers, through the firm and on to customers.[1]

Logistics is thus concerned with the management of the physical flow which begins with sources of supply and ends at the point of consumption. It is clearly therefore much wider in its reach than simply a concern with the movement of finished goods – a commonly held view of physical distribution. Logistics is just as much concerned with plant and depot location, inventory levels, materials management and information systems as with transport.

One of the features of the logistics concept which is its greatest attraction whilst simultaneously being the greatest drawback to its widespread adoption in industry so far is that it places the emphasis on integrating activities that traditionally have been located in different functions of the business. For example, in many companies responsibility for inventory and transport may be vested in the production and distribution functions respectively and decisions on one will often be made without regard for the

1

other. The logistics viewpoint however forces the decision-taker to recognise the connections between the component elements of the materials flow system, indeed it encourages comprehensive systems thinking rather than functional tunnel vision.

It is interesting to trace the evolution of thought in the logistics activity and then to assess its importance for business today. As early as 1915, writing from Harvard Business School, Arch Shaw took a view of logistics which was radically far-sighted:

> The relations between the activities of demand creation and physical supply . . . illustrate the existence of the two principles of interdependence and balance. Failure to co-ordinate any one of these activities with its group-fellows and also with those in the other group, or undue emphasis or outlay put upon any one of these activities, is certain to upset the equilibrium of forces which means efficient distribution. . . . The physical distribution of the goods is a problem distinct from the creation of demand . . . Not a few worthy failures in distribution campaigns have been due to such a lack of co-ordination between demand creation and physical supply . . . Instead of being a subsequent problem, this question of supply must be met and answered before the work of distribution begins.[2]

This view of logistics as a bridge beween demand creation and physical supply is still as valid today as it was when first expressed 70 years ago. No matter how fundamental this idea was, very little attention seems to have been paid to it and indeed in 1962 one of the gurus of management, Peter Drucker, writing in *Fortune* magazine said: 'Physical distribution is today's frontier in business. It is one area where managerial results of great magnitude can be achieved. And it is still largely unexplored territory'.[3] There are signs however that management consciousness of the importance of logistics is growing and the last ten years have seen a major upsurge in interest in this area.

A number of factors have contributed to this growth in interest. One of these is that inevitably as companies seek out areas for productivity improvement they are forced to confront the major source of corporate costs represented by distribution. Production and marketing have both been subjected to scrutiny by academic commentators and the more efficiency-conscious companies. Now it is the turn of the materials flow system that binds production and marketing to receive similar examination.

Giving increased urgency to this examination is the growth in the costs of movement and storage. Energy crises have had a direct impact upon transport costs and soaring interest rates have greatly increased the costs of holding stocks. Beyond this the vast proliferation in the size of most companies' product ranges has meant that the total stockholding investment of these companies has increased dramatically. For example, ten years ago Birds Eye offered a range of only 200 items compared with its present range of over 500 items, which illustrates how important a factor in the corporate balance sheet inventory now is.

Changes in the channels of distribution have forced many manufacturers and distributors to take a fresh look at their distribution systems. Grocery retailing in the UK is a prominent example of how power in the marketing channel has dramatically changed hands. Twenty-five years ago there were 150,000 retail grocery outlets; today there are only 68,000. Clearly the size of these outlets in physical and turnover terms has increased considerably and so too has the centralisation of retail buying power. For example Tesco and Sainsbury together account for over 25 per cent of the UK sales of groceries. The impact on manufacturers and in particular on their distribution systems has been far reaching. Similar changes in channel relationships have occurred in many other industries too.

The combination of all these factors has brought the distribution problem into sharp focus. Awareness is growing both of the impact of logistics upon corporate profitability and, underlying this, its impact upon the national economy.

Logistics and the national economy

Logistics pervades almost every facet of economic activity. It provides the network whereby our everyday life is supported.

In the developed economies it is typically the case that one-third of the Gross Domestic Product is accounted for by the distribution sector. For example one study[4] reported that in the UK distribution represented 32.5 per cent of GDP. Studies in other countries reveal a similar magnitude of activity. Thus in terms of cost alone logistics activities account for a massive part of total national expenditure.

Clearly any productivity improvement that could be achieved in any part of the logistics system would release resources for use elsewhere in the economy. A study[5] recently commissioned by the National Council of Physical Distribution Management in the USA suggested that effective productivity improvement programmes in logistics could lead to reductions of between 10 and 20 per cent in total corporate costs. There is strong evidence to suggest that similar savings are potentially available in other developed economies; in some cases the savings could be considerably higher.

It should not be imagined, however, that logistics activity is merely a cost and as such the only desirable course of action is to reduce it. On the contrary, logistics is a positive contributor to national wealth. It facilitates the economic process and in many ways it is the engine that drives that process.

The concept of logistics management

The logistics concept is based on a total systems view of the materials and goods flow activity from the source of supply through to the final point of consumption. It recognises the interconnections and interrelationships between the multitude of functions involved in this movement from source to user and in so doing forces management to think in terms of managing the total system rather than just one part of it.

The specific functional areas that are encompassed by logistics might be termed the 'logistics mix' and could be summarised as follows:

> Inventory
> e.g. – Service level decisions
>   – Materials requirements planning
> Information
> e.g. – Order processing
>   – Demand forecasting
> Warehousing and handling
> e.g. – Depot location
>   – Unitisation and packaging
> Transport
> e.g. – Mode decisions
>   – Scheduling

The logistics management task is concerned with the integration and co-ordination of these activities in such a way that end markets are served in the most cost effective manner.

The whole purpose of logistics is to provide 'availability'. Everyone will be familiar with the old cliché: 'The right product in the right place at the right time'. If one adds 'at the least cost' then that is precisely the objective of logistics management.

Another way of defining the objective could be in terms of

'customer service', which is simply an elaboration on the notion of 'availability'. The idea of customer service encompasses all the points of contact between the customer and the supplier in terms of physical fulfilment of orders. Customer service is the output of the logistics system and it results from the combined effects of the activity centres within the 'logistics mix'. All these activities are important in establishing a desired level of customer service performance. They are also interdependent; if one activity fails, the system fails, creating poor performance, and destabilising workloads in other areas, resulting in poor cost effectiveness for the system as a whole. A failure in sales forecasting may influence materials requirements planning which then results in low product availability of finished goods inventory. This in turn may either result in lost sales or an increased number of back orders which may in turn delay order processing and hence extend the order cycle time. This may result in the need to expedite shipments which increases the cost of service to the customer.[6]

It will be apparent that the provision of improved customer service will normally incur additional costs for the company. The higher the level of service offered the higher will be the costs. In fact it can be shown that once the level of service increases beyond the 70-80 per cent mark, the associated costs increase far more than proportionately ('service level' being defined for our purposes as the percentage of orders that can be met from stock within a given period).

The implications of this cost function for the distributing company are worth some attention. In the first place, many companies, far from having any laid down service policy, are totally unaware of the level of service at which they are operating. Even if the company does have a declared service policy it is often the case that service levels have been arbitrarily set. The effect of offering a 97 per cent level of service instead of a 95 per cent level may have only a slight effect on customer demand, yet it will have a considerable effect on distribution costs. For normally distributed demand this 2 per cent increase in the level of service would lead to a 14 per cent increase in safety stock.

Therefore it is essential that management recognises the cost implications of a service strategy. Indeed by offering logistics service the firm is absorbing a cost that would otherwise have to be borne by the customer. For example, if the supplying company delivers twice a week instead of once a week, they are relieving their customer of a certain responsibility for holding stock – the more frequent the deliveries, the less stock the customer needs to hold. Similarly, if the customer knows that when he orders an item from that supplier, the supplier will rarely be out of stock and can deliver it speedily to him, then again the customer's stockholding can be lower. Because it costs money to hold stock – currently about 25 per cent of its value a year – the supplier is absorbing this customer cost by his service offering.

What are the costs of distribution?

There has been a tendency in the past for companies to consider only the costs of transport and, perhaps, warehouses as constituting their distribution costs. Recently more companies have adopted the 'total distribution cost' concept in relation to their distribution activity. This concept recognises that many more costs are incurred through the provision of availability than just transport and warehouse costs. For example, decisions about service level, as has been seen, affect the amount of inventory that needs to be held in the system; thus the cost of holding inventory must be included as a distribution cost. Likewise, order processing costs are clearly influenced by the distribution activity, so they must be included as well; indeed there is also a case for including invoicing costs. The costs of materials handling and protective packaging should also form part of the total distribution cost, as well as the costs of managing and administering the distribution system.

The total distribution cost concept in the form of an equation may be expressed as follows:

$$TDC = TC + FC + CC + IC + HC + PC + MC$$

where

TDC = Total distribution costs
TC = Transport costs
FC = Facilities costs (depots, warehouses etc.)
CC = Communications costs (order processing invoicing etc.)
IC = Inventory cost
HC = Materials handling costs
PC = Protective packing costs
MC = Distribution management costs

Various surveys have been made of the relative costs of distribution in industry and their findings seem to suggest that, on average, the costs represent about 15 per cent of sales turnover for a typical company. Averages can be misleading and, depending on the nature of the business, the figures can be very much higher or lower. Table 1.1 shows a large food company's analysis of its total distribution costs. Whilst this company has placed some costs under slightly different headings from those used in the TDC formula above, they amount to the same thing in total.

Table 1.1
Total distribution costs (expressed as a percentage of total sales)

Transport inwards		
Materials to factories		1.0
Transport outwards		
Palletisation	0.02	
Factories to depots	1.71	
Depots to customer	2.09	3.82
Warehouses, depots		
Clerical wages	0.16	
Warehouse labour	1.29	
Other costs	1.19	2.64
Order processing		
Rental of terminals	0.11	
Operating terminals	0.07	
Computer	0.03	
Sales accounting	0.68	0.89
Protective packaging		2.00
Management		
Management costs	0.17	
Stock auditing	0.02	
Stock planning	0.01	
Training	0.01	0.21
Stock losses		0.26
Interest on capital		
Stocks	0.24	
Building, vehicles, plant	0.46	0.70
Total		11.52

One of the benefits of being able to identify the specific sources of total distribution costs is that it becomes easier to identify potential 'trade-offs'. A trade-off occurs where an increased cost in one area is more than matched by a cost reduction in another area, thus leading to an improved situation overall. Thus a distribution system with ten regional depots has high warehouse and stockholding costs compared with a system of only five depots, but the savings on trunk haulage and the reduction of stock-outs may more than compensate for the extra costs involved in the ten depot system. In this case, an increase in warehouse and stock carrying costs has been traded-off against a reduction in total system costs.

Generally, the effects of trade-offs are assessed in two ways: first from the point of view of their impact on total system costs, and second from their impact on sales revenue. It is possible to trade-off costs in such a way that total costs increase, yet because of the better service now being offered, sales revenue increases. If the difference between revenue and costs is greater than before, the trade-off may be regarded as leading to an improvement in cost effectiveness.

In addition to the possibility of trading-off costs between the various elements in the distribution system, e.g. between depot costs and stockholding costs, there is the possibility of identifying trade-offs within an individual element. Thus, stock levels of finished goods in the logistics system may be reduced at the expense of the level of service offered, but the reduction in sales revenue resulting is more than compensated for by the reduction in stockholding costs, or vice versa in different circumstances.

Total systems management

For the benefits of such trade-offs to be fully achieved it is necessary for managers to begin to think in terms of total systems rather than of narrow functional areas. A great deal has been written and talked about systems, systems approaches, systems thinking and systems management. Whilst as a generalisation it would probably be correct to define anything that converts an input into an output as a 'system', the concept of a logistics system is rather more complex. We have seen that the logistics system in its totality is concerned with the movement and storage of products from their raw state, through various stages of sub-assembly, manufacture, packaging, transportation and delivery to the final customer. Depending upon how widely one defines the 'system' it can be seen that logistics considerations are involved throughout the marketing and exchange channel from the sources of supply to the points of final consumption. To add to the complexity it is unlikely that the same corporate entity will be involved, or will have control, over the entire system. Furthermore, within the company itself many functional areas, or subsystems, will exist which may have conflicting goals or objectives.

This latter feature is of particular concern to logistics systems management. Table 1.2 shows some of the conflicts that can occur between functions of the firm (i.e. subsystems) when goals are determined by functions without regard for the impact of their actions upon the total system. This very common feature of corporate structures is called by the operations researchers 'suboptimisation', in other words a failure to recognise that, unless carefully managed, the whole can sometimes be less than the sum of its parts.

As we shall see later in this book when the organisational implications of logistics are discussed, the ultimate rationale of the logistics concept is to reduce suboptimisation within the firm through a greater integration and coordination of connected activities. Figure 1.1 represents the materials and information flows that must be managed to provide cost effective customer service.

Many companies fail to recognise that the material flow through the firm and the related flow of information (i.e. orders, forecasts, stock reports etc.) should most logically be seen as an integrated system. Typically responsibility for the various functions involved in those flows is fragmented. At best there will be a partial attempt at integration through the development of a materials management function to manage goods inwards and the procurement of materials and a parallel distribution management function responsible for the delivery of finished goods. The logistics concept suggests that greater efficiency and effectiveness can be achieved through an even wider, total systems view.

There are signs that some companies are moving towards the adoption of such an approach to logistics management. Indeed it has been suggested that there is a process of 'evolution' by which the firm might progress on its way to the adoption of a logistics orientation. There are three stages, namely:

Transport management

In this very basic situation the organisation will not have recognised the function of transport except as a means of moving the product from the factory or warehouse to the customer's premises. It will be viewed as a purely mechanical task which does not need senior management attention. Often it will be managed by personnel with little status in the organisation and no attempt will have been made to integrate the transport activity with other demand fulfilling tasks such as warehousing, order processing and

Table 1.2
Situations which can give rise to inter-departmental conflicts

Subsystems goal	Purchasing	Production	Finance	Marketing	Logistics
Bulk purchases of materials	Advantage: larger discounts		Disadvantage: working capital tied up		Disadvantage: warehousing costs increased
Long production runs		Advantage: low costs	Disadvantage: working capital tied up	Disadvantage: narrow product range	Disadvantage: warehousing costs increased
Broad product range	Disadvantage: discounts small on low volume purchases	Disadvantage: short, high cost runs	Disadvantage: finished goods stocks high	Advantage: more sales through wider customer appeal	Disadvantage: higher costs through more administration and more warehousing space
Tighter credit control			Advantage: greater use of working capital	Disadvantage: possible loss of sales	
4 day delivery (from 7 days)			Disadvantage: higher operating costs	Advantage: more sales because of better service	Disadvantage: system costs increased in order to meet service requirements
Unit loads			Advantage: lower operating costs	Disadvantage: loss of sales to small customers	Advantage: system costs can be lowered by eliminating uneconomic calls

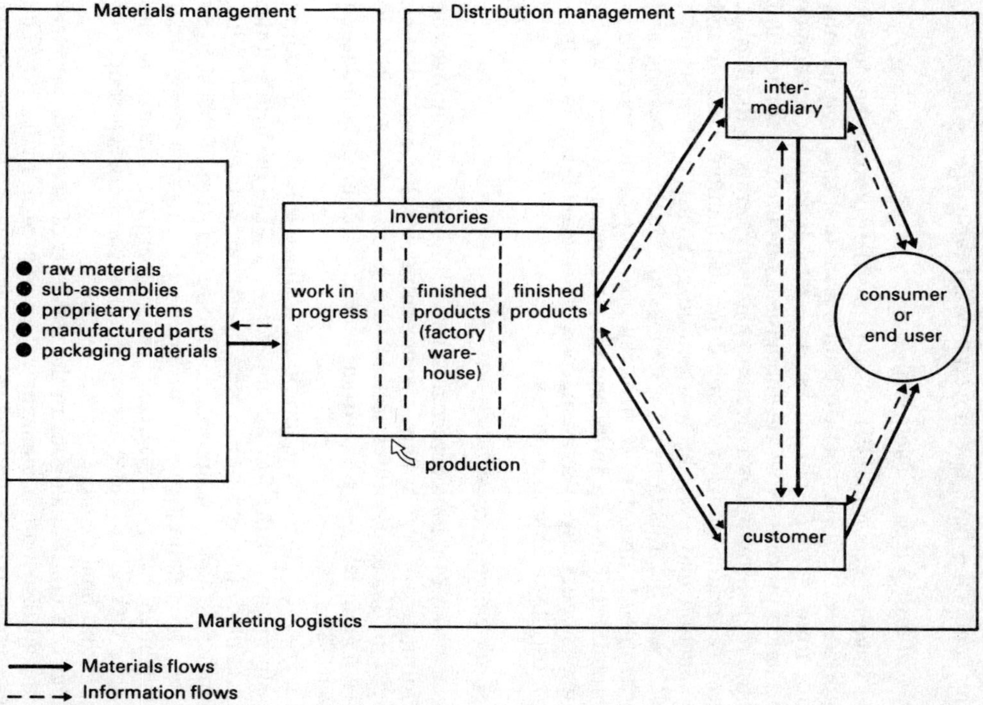
Materials management
Distribution management
raw materials
sub-assemblies
proprietary items
manufactured parts
packaging materials
Inventories
work in progress
finished products (factory ware-house)
finished products
production
inter-mediary
customer
consumer or end user
Marketing logistics
Materials flows
Information flows

Figure 1.1 The logistics systems concept

inventory control. The emphasis will be on cost minimisation, with the transport function being evaluated in terms of cost per mile or cost per case shipped or some such similar measure. Unfortunately many companies have not moved beyond this stage.

Physical distribution management

This stage reflects a major transition for the company because it requires a recognition that distribution is more than simply moving goods from *A* to *B*, but instead is a vital link in the customer satisfaction process. Now the emphasis is on customer service and the use of distribution as a means of gaining leverage in the market place. A greater status is accorded the distribution manager and the function may even be represented at board level in its own right. Now the functions of warehousing, order processing and finished goods inventory control will probably be incorporated in the total distribution activity and the performance criteria will be as much about delivery as about costs. This second stage is perhaps the most observable in industry today.

Logistics management

The logistics orientation recognises that in order to improve the performance of the system, as measured by the cost effective provision of customer service, all the interrelated activities in moving materials and goods from source to user must be managed as a whole.

Clearly the logistics concept as defined involves a radical transformation of the way a company faces up to the needs of the market place in terms of its entire operations management. What is implicit in this new approach is the recognition of the need to balance the requirements of customer service against the internal management of its resources. The integrative nature of the logistics task is to bridge the operations gap between source of supply and final demand.

This concept is analogous to the concepts of materials management and distribution management presented in figure 1.1. The suggestion here is that logistics is a planning framework rather than a business function. In other words the management task inherent in logistics is not so much concerned with the management of materials flows but rather with providing the mechanism for establishing objectives and strategies within which the day-to-day activities of materials management and distribution management can take place.

The main theme of this book is that logistics must be recognised by management as a total business planning orientation. It affects the balance sheet and the profit and loss account, it has implications for resource utilisation and it can provide the means for coordinating supply, operations and distribution. What it cannot do, except in the very simplest of organisations, is provide a means of managing the entire business.

Notes

1   An amended version of the definition given by D. Bowersox in *Logistics Mannagement*, 2nd edition, Macmillan, 1978.
2   A. W. Shaw, *Some Problems in Market Distribution*, Harvard University Press, 1915.
3   P. Drucker, 'The Economy's Dark Continent' in *Fortune*, vol. 72, April 1962.
4   A. Childerley, 'The Importance of Logistics in the UK Economy' in *International Journal of Physical Distribution and Materials Management*, vol. 10, no. 8, 1980.
5   National Council of Physical Distribution Management, *Measuring Productivity in Physical Distribution*, NCPDM, 1978.
6   M. Christopher, P. Schary and T. Skjott-Larsen, *Customer Service and Distribution Strategy*, Associated Business Press, 1979.

2   The corporate role of logistics

Many companies fail to recognise the impact that improvements in logistics management can make both on the achievement of their strategic goals and also on their financial performance. As will be seen in Chapter 3, logistics can play a central part in determining the market share a company is able to gain at the expense of competition. Similarly, logistics orientation can bring about major improvements in operations management through the more effective use of resources. The combined effect of these factors is reflected in both the company's balance sheet and its profit and loss account.

Those managements that have adopted the logistics concept and have built logistical considerations into their strategy formulation have often seen quite dramatic improvements in their overall return on investment (ROI). The double-edged impact of logistics in bringing about both increased market share and reduced costs on a lower asset base can provide a substantial source of leverage on ROI. Let us examine this effect in more detail.

Return on investment is a convenient measure of a company's financial performance, particularly when plotted over a period of time. It reflects the extent to which the organisation is effectively deploying its assets and is efficient in its management of those assets. The assets of a business are conveniently categorised as 'fixed' and 'current' and the firm's logistics activity can be a heavy user of both. For example plants, warehouses, vehicles, materials handling equipment etc., if owned by the business, are part of its fixed assets. Likewise current assets, which comprise inventory, accounts receivables (less accounts payable) and cash, are also very much affected by logistics decisions.

Figure 2.1 illustrates the key components of ROI and it is worth noting the specific ways in which logistics can affect the separate elements in the relationship.

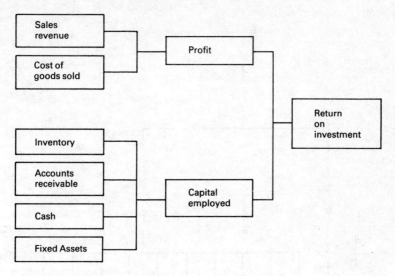

Figure 2.1 The components of ROI

Logistics profit contribution

Figure 2.2 identifies the way in which revenue and cost are affected by logistics. Taking each element in turn the impact of logistics can be identified:

Net sales

The effectiveness or otherwise with which the company offers a competitive level of customer service can have a major impact on market share (see Chapter 3).

Cost of goods sold

Improvements in the integration of the procurement function with production planning, which should be one of the benefits of logistical coordination, will result in greater economies in purchasing and in production (see Chapter 7).

Selling and administrative expense

In the context of logistics the relevant costs under this heading are those associated with 'filling orders'. Thus the costs of order processing, transport, warehousing, inventory control, protective

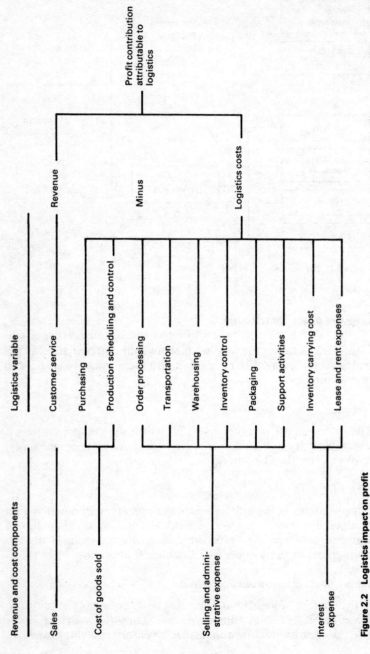

Figure 2.2 Logistics impact on profit

16

packaging and support activities (e.g. spare parts, after sales service etc.) must be included here. The problems of identifying these costs are examined in Chapter 4.

Interest expense

All too often these costs are not treated as logistics expenses. However the cost of holding inventory is clearly attributable to logistics decisions and therefore must be included, particularly as in a high interest rate environment it becomes a major item. Whilst strictly speaking lease and rental costs are not 'interest expenses' they are included here for convenience. Again they are becoming a major cost for many companies.

The combined impact of these influences on revenue and cost might be termed the 'profit contribution attributable to logistics'. Whilst there are many problems concerning the effect of customer service on revenue it is a valuable concept to focus upon, if only to reduce the widespread tendency to see logistics as a cost centre rather than a profit centre. This is particularly important given the understandable response of managers to cost centres, which is 'how can costs be reduced?'. Whilst cost reduction in any area of the business is a worthy objective it is only desirable if it leads to profit improvement. In logistics, as elsewhere, both the revenue effects and the cost effects of decisions must be carefully assessed. Whether logistics can be managed as a profit centre is an issue to which we shall return later.

The logistics asset base

The second dimension influencing ROI is the investment itself, sometimes referred to as capital employed or the asset base. The management of this asset base is just as important as the management of profit contribution, yet there are many examples of poor control of assets, particularly current assets, which lead to reduced return on investment. One area where better control can provide worthwhile improvements is inventory management. As shown in Chapter 4 the costs of holding inventory are high, for most companies something like 25 per cent per annum of its value is realistic. The following example shows the leverage effect on return on investment brought about by a reduction in inventory in one particular company.

Assumptions:
      25 per cent of total capital employed is in inventory

50 per cent of total inventory is in finished goods (i.e. 12.5 per cent of total assets)

Current ROI = 20 per cent

Carrying cost of inventory = 25 per cent

Improved inventory management policies and procedures reduce finished goods investment by 25 per cent

Carrying cost of finished goods inventory = 3.125 per cent of total (i.e. 25 per cent of 12.5 per cent)

$$\text{Now ROI} = \frac{20\% + (25\% \times 3.125\%)}{100\% - (25\% \times 12.5\%)}$$

$$= 22\%$$

This example of improved ROI through better management of logistics assets is particularly interesting because reductions in inventory will effect both profits and investment thus giving an extra boost to ROI. Profits are improved as a result of reduced inventory carrying costs and total capital employed is reduced by the value of the inventory saved.

Figure 2.3 summarises the major category of assets and liabilities as they would appear on the company's balance sheet.

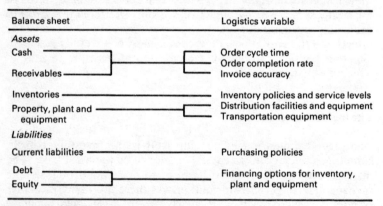

Figure 2.3   Logistics impact on balance sheet

By examining each element of the balance sheet in turn it will be seen how logistics variables can influence its final shape.

Cash and receivables

This component of current assets is crucial to the liquidity of the business. In recent years its importance has been recognised as more companies become squeezed for cash. It is not always recognised however that logistics variables have a direct impact on this part of the balance sheet. For example the shorter the order cycle time, from when the customer places the order to when the goods are delivered, the sooner the invoice can be issued. Likewise the order completion rate can affect the cash flow if the invoice is not issued until after the goods are despatched. One of the less obvious logistics variables affecting cash and receivables is invoice accuracy. If the customer finds that his invoice is inaccurate he is unlikely to pay and the payment lead time will be extended until the problem is rectified.

Inventories

Fifty per cent or more of a company's current assets will often be tied up in inventory. Logistics is concerned with all inventory within the business from raw materials, sub-assembly or bought in components, through work-in-progress to finished goods. The company's policies on inventory levels and stock locations will clearly influence the size of total inventory. Also influential will be the extent to which inventory levels are monitored and managed and beyond that the extent to which systems are in operation which minimise the requirements for inventory. Systems such as distribution requirements planning, DRP (see Chapter 7), can have a major impact on the total inventory in the system.

Property, plant and equipment

The logistics system of any business will usually be a heavy user of fixed assets. The plant, depots and warehouses which form the logistics network if valued realistically on a replacement basis will represent a substantial part of total capital employed (assuming that they are owned rather than rented or leased). Materials handling equipment, vehicles and other equipment involved in storage and transport can also add considerably to the total sum of fixed assets. Many companies fail to recognise the true significance of logistics fixed assets because they are valued for balance sheet purposes at historical cost. Warehouses, for example, with their associated storage and handling equipment represent a sizeable investment and the question should be asked: 'Is this the most effective way to deploy our assets?'

Current liabilities

The current liabilities of the business are debts which must be paid in cash within a specified period of time. From the logistics point of view the key elements are accounts payable for bought in materials, components etc. This is an area where a greater integration of purchasing with operations management can yield dividends. The traditional concepts of economic orders can often lead to excessive levels of raw materials inventory as those quantities may not reflect manufacturing or distribution requirements. The phasing of supplies to match the total logistics requirements of the system can be achieved through the twin techniques of materials requirements planning (MRP) and distribution requirements planning (DRP) (see Chapter 7). If premature commitment of materials can be minimised this should lead to an improved position on current liabilities.

Debt/equity

Whilst the balance between debt and equity has many ramifications for the financial management of the total business it is worth reflecting on the impact of alternative logistics strategies. More companies are leasing plant facilities and equipment and thus converting a fixed asset into a continuing expense. The growing use of third-party operations for warehousing and transport instead of providing these facilities in-house is a parallel development. These changes obviously affect the funding requirements of the business. They may also affect the means whereby that funding is achieved, i.e. through debt rather than equity. The ratio of debt to equity, usually referred to as 'gearing' or 'leverage', will influence the return on equity and will also have implications for cash flow in terms of interest payments and debt repayment.

Improving ROI through logistics management

The foregoing analysis shows that logistics management influences almost every aspect of the company's profit and loss account and its balance sheet. Changes in logistics policy and strategy will work their way through the business and affect financial performance and indeed will contribute in a major way to the long-term viability of the firm. Therefore the business should constantly review its logistics strategy and its deployment of logistics assets to ensure that maximum productivity of resources is achieved. For example, where the company owns its own fixed logistics assets the question should be asked: 'Is the level of utilisation as high as possible?'. An audit of these facilities will often reveal levels of utilisation well below their maximum capacity – in many cases because of poor space management within the warehouse or less than optimal vehicle routing and load planning.

One large British company operating its own distribution system in the UK found that computerised scheduling and routing methods can achieve a 20 per cent reduction in the number of vehicles required and a fuel saving of 15 per cent. As the company was using between three and four million gallons of diesel and petrol a year, such a saving is of some significance.

Again many companies have benefited from reviewing their plant and depot policy, both in terms of numbers and locations. Depot networks established fifteen years ago may not look so attractive in today's cost environment. While all costs have increased, the differing relative increases in fuel costs, interest charges and labour rates could radically change our views on the appropriateness of the existing policy. For example many large UK brewing companies have developed their businesses over the last 20 years around the acquisition of smaller units with a subsequent centralisation of brewing and distribution facilities. Technological innovation enabled beer to be brewed most economically in larger central units and then transported over large distances without any subsequent loss in product quality. Cost analyses at the time demonstrated that the overwhelming production advantages outweighed any minor distribution disadvantages. Now the cost of transport relative to the cost of brewing has increased substantially and the breweries who supply on a regional basis are often able to show a greater return on assets than the larger, centralised brewers.

The following formula is worth keeping in mind:

$$\text{Return on investment} = \frac{\text{Profit}}{\text{Sales}} \times \frac{\text{Sales}}{\text{Capital}}$$
$$(\text{ROI})$$

It will be seen that ROI is the product of two ratios: the first, profit:sales, being commonly referred to as the *margin* and the second, sales:capital, termed *capital turnover*. Thus to gain improvement in ROI one or other or both of these ratios must increase. Since in the recent economic conditions there has been continuing pressure on margins, the only hope of maintaining an adequate ROI for many companies is to improve capital turnover. However, if one were to plot the ratio of capital to sales in the company as a whole over a period of time the startling result is that it often turns out to be fairly constant. Thus even when sales value increases so, it seems, does total capital employed.

Figure 2.4 shows that this particular company has consistently had a capital turnover of less than 1 even with sales growth. In

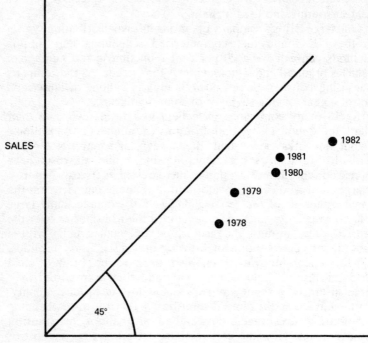

Figure 2.4   Capital turnover

other words whatever the size of the margin, its effect on ROI is being reduced as a result of the low capital turnover. To gain a positive leverage effect on ROI the ratio of sales:capital must be greater than 1.

It has been shown that more effective logistics management can be one way of improving the utilisation of assets and thus, in effect, of improving capital turnover.

Logistics in corporate strategy

It is often forgotten that there is a major role for logistics in the development of corporate strategy. Instead a narrow cost-reduction focus is adopted and as a result many opportunities for improved market performance are missed. Increasingly, however, the more sophisticated organisations are recognising that logistics has a wider role to play within the business. Decisions taken now on distribution networks, management of materials flow and information systems can be crucial in determining the ability of the company to respond to changed market circumstances or new business opportunities.

A good example of how logistics can affect the highest level is provided by the example of SKF, the Swedish bearings manufacturer. Several years ago SKF was facing severe competition in its European markets from Japanese suppliers who were able to supply standard bearings at a price not much higher than SKF's production cost. Analysis of the situation highlighted the fact that whilst SKF was producing over 50,000 variants the Japanese were concentrating on a very limited range of fast-moving lines. Moreover SKF had plants in Sweden, Germany, UK, France and Italy each of which was generally providing the full range of variants. Thus it became clear that SKF was unable to gain the benefits of scale at the production level because the typical batch run length was so small. The Japanese on the other hand were mass-producing a much smaller number of items and as a consequence were much lower down the 'experience curve', which was reflected in their lower costs.

SKF's response was essentially logistical. It firstly reviewed its product range with the object of substantially reducing the number of items manufactured. Beyond this however it decided to concentrate the production of certain categories of bearings at individual manufacturing locations. Thus the French factory would produce bearings which would only be produced there, Italy had its own unique line and similarly at each of its other manufacturing locations.

The end result was a classic trade-off in logistics costs. On the one hand the costs of transport involved in distributing finished produce from the plant in, say, Sweden to a customer in the UK were substantially higher than hitherto when that customer had been supplied from the UK. On the other hand the production cost savings more than offset this extra cost.

The company installed a sophisticated information and planning system which enabled a centralised control of production and the allocation of inventory to local stocking points. This system, which it called the global forecasting and supply system (GFSS) is essentially a logistics management system.

Whilst SKF has faced recent severe trading conditions due to recession in its major markets it is probably true to say that its position would be much worse if it were not for the adoption of this radical approach to logistics management.

In a quite different context one of North America's largest

wholesale distributors, Foremost-McKesson, revised its logistics strategy to rescue a fast-deteriorating profit situation. The company was faced with a classic 'middleman squeeze' with more manufacturers delivering direct to the retailer. The company's response was to seek additional ways in which it could 'add value' to the basic distribution process.[1] Amongst Foremost's responses to the situation were:

–   Taking waste products as well as finished goods from chemical manufacturers, and recycling the wastes through its own plants – its first entry into chemical waste management.
–   Creating a massive merchandising service by providing teams to set up displays of manufacturers' goods within stores.
–   Acting as middleman between drug stores and insurance offices by processing medical consumer claims.
–   Using the information from its computer to help manufacturers manage inventories, collect and analyse market data, and even plan sales and new product development.
–   Leasing electronic ordering equipment to retailers, offering shelf management plans, and even providing price labels.

These and other actions have transformed the company's profitability, which has been achieved by the recognition that logistics is essentially a strategic orientation.

One further example underlines the positive impact on the market place that a well thought through logistics strategy can achieve. The Whirlpool Corporation is a major US manufacturer of domestic appliances such as washing machines, spin dryers etc. To give some idea of its size the company estimates that every day approximately 25,000 customers buy one or more of its appliances. A significant percentage of these appliances are purchased from 900 Sears retail stores and 1,700 Sears catalogue outlets, and a further proportion is purchased from 13,500 franchised Whirlpool Brand retail and builder outlets which are supplied from 45 wholesale distributors. As might be imagined the logistics of supplying these various channels of distribution from eight manufacturing facilities located in six different states are extremely complex. The company estimates that its daily shipments throughout the system are equivalent to a freight train seven miles long!

It was recognised some years ago that in a competitive marketplace product availability and customer choice were highly important. Yet given the size of Whirlpool's product range the cost of holding high levels of inventory throughout the channel would be prohibitive. To solve this problem the company has installed a 'real-time' inventory control and order processing system. If a customer walks into a Sears retail store on, say, Monday and selects a model it can be in his home by Thursday. The way it works is that on Monday evening all the orders for Whirlpool products from that store are transmitted to the nearest Sears regional distribution centre (RDC). On Tuesday morning the RDC combines all orders from its assigned retail stores and transmits its total needs directly into Whirlpool's computer which processes the order, reserves inventory and transmits a shipping document to the appropriate Whirlpool distribution centre by Tuesday afternoon. That same afternoon or evening a trailer is loaded for delivery overnight to the Sears RDC early Wednesday morning from where it is broken into local delivery routes for delivery to the customer's home the following day.

The effect of this is to minimise the total inventory in the system. Apart from the items held in the retail store, which are for display purposes only, the only place inventory is held is in the nineteen Whirlpool distribution centres. Not only is inventory reduced through this consolidation but also vehicle space utilisation is maximised by shipping complete trailer loads to Sears' warehouses. A further sophistication that has recently been introduced is to offer a greater range of colours for appliances but not to hold all these colours in stock. Instead orders are consolidated by colour and unpainted appliances (which are held in stock) are then sprayed the appropriate colour. This postponement of the commitment to colour allows a further substantial reduction in total stockholding.

The end result of these logistical decisions has been to enhance the customer service both in terms of speedy availability and choice and to improve Whirlpool's market position.

A number of generalised principles can be derived from the three examples given above. In the case of SKF the benefits came through rationalisation and standardisation, with Foremost-McKesson the development of a specialised third party distribution concept produced substantial marketing improvement and Whirlpool's success in offering higher levels of customer service at lower cost came through consolidation and postponement of the commitment of inventory.

Rationalisation and standardisation

Many companies have experienced a substantial increase in the number of stockkeeping units (SKUs) over the last twenty years or so. This has come about through the proliferation and extension of product lines. For example, when Bowaters first entered the kitchen paper tissue market it offered a very limited range of kitchen rolls, but it now produces them in a variety of colours and patterns, in different pack sizes and under a number of brand names. Each one of these combinations represents a separate stockkeeping unit and a separate inventory must be maintained for each.

Whilst there are many arguments in favour of such a product range extension from a marketing point of view, there are also substantial cost penalties for following such a strategy. New companies are taking a much harder look at their product ranges to seek ways of reducing the slow moving lines. The same pressure is also making those companies review their range of customer accounts to identify the true costs of providing service to different customer types (see Chapter 4).

Underlying this pressure for rationalisation is the so-called 80/20 or Pareto rule. Pareto was a nineteenth-century Italian economist who examined the distribution of wealth in Italy and discovered that 80 per cent of the country's total wealth was in the ownership of only 20 per cent of the population. Subsequently this 80/20 rule has been found to apply across a vast range of situations. In particular it seems that in almost every business 80 per cent of the total turnover of the business will come from just 20 per cent of the product range. Similarly 80 per cent of the total turnover will come from only 20 per cent of the customers.

It is a valuable exercise to look at the company's product range in this way and identify which products are the fast movers and which move more slowly in terms of turnover. Ideally the same analysis should also be performed by profitability as turnover and profitability need not necessarily be related. Figure 2.5 shows the type of picture which would emerge from such an analysis.

This could be the basis for an 'ABC' analysis indicating which products should be given lower priority in terms of service, i.e. reduced inventory holdings on the slower moving lines. The analysis could also direct management's attention to those products which could be removed from the range altogether, as in the SKF example above. Such a policy should be implemented with great care to ensure that the company does not discard products unless either they are making a loss or there is an 'opportunity cost' in terms of the resources they absorb. A judicious programme of product rationalisation will have a marked impact upon the total inventory in the system and upon the storage requirement and should lead to improved profitability.

The idea of standardisation is closely linked to rationalisation.

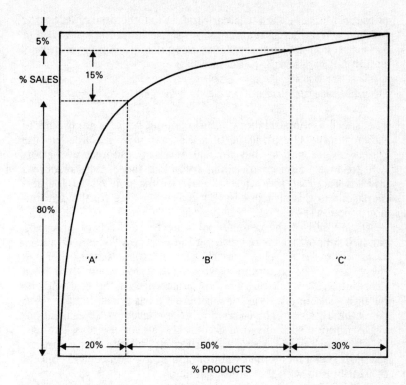

Figure 2.5   80/20 Analysis of product range

Here the search should be for the reduction in non-standard versions of range items. Again not carried out blindly without regard for market impact, but rather with a view to directing customers to other range items. SKF found it was able to do this quite successfully, particularly when customers found that the standard items were substantially cheaper than the non-standard.

The same principle of standardisation should also be applied where possible to parts, components and materials. A company such as Philips, manufacturing a wide variety of electrical goods, has found that by utilising a greater number of common components and sub-assemblies its total inventory of those items can be greatly reduced.

The benefits of rationalisation and standardisation can also be extended as a result of the 'experience effect', a well documented phenomenon.[2] Based upon the earlier idea of the 'learning curve' it suggests that as a company achieves a greater accumulation in output (volume) on a particular product line the total costs of that product will reduce in real terms. As a generalisation it seems that for every doubling in cumulative output real average unit costs should fall by 20 to 30 per cent.

Distribution specialisation

The 'specialisation of labour' is an economic concept going back to Adam Smith. The principle of specialisation is grounded in the commonsense notion that concentration of resources and effort will produce better results than spreading those same resources and efforts over too wide a field. In the context of logistics management this principle has special significance for the distribution function.

At one end of the commercial scale there are companies too small to support a national distribution system yet who need such a system in order to achieve market penetration. At the other end there are large companies who have established their own distribution network but who are concerned at the cost and the balance sheet implications of substantial fixed assets. In both these cases the answer might be found in the concept of specialisation.

Distribution specialisation is coming to mean one of two things. Firstly it means the use of a 'third party' distribution company, secondly it can mean the establishment of a 'profit centre' concept of distribution with the parent company.

The rapid growth of 'third party' specialist distribution companies in the UK since the war has partly come about through a greater freedom from legal regulation than was the case until just recently, for example, in the United States. Transport companies have been able to expand their activities into storage, inventory management and even order processing and to adopt a very flexible, market-oriented approach to price. In effect these companies are offering a 'shared service'[3] which means that the high level of fixed costs necessary to the operation of a national distribution system is spread amongst many users.

The advantages to a company of 'contracting out' its distribution to a specialist operator are basically related to the economies of scale, through consolidation of movements and storage, that can be achieved by the specialist distribution company. Even a major manufacturing company may not be able to match the unit costs of transport and storage, and the regularity and reliability of delivery, that can be achieved by specialist service companies like Cory, Unilever's SPD, or British Road Services.

It may be objected that problems will arise as a result of loss of control over distribution if third party operators are used, but these fears are seldom fully justified. In any case, any problems that might develop are quite likely to be overshadowed by the transformation of the return on investment following the reduction in fixed assets. This logistics decision can be likened to a manufacturer's 'make or buy' decision: should the company do its own distribution or should it buy in either all or part of its requirements? Studies have recently been conducted to appraise the costs and benefits of contracting out distribution to a specialist service company.[4] The main advantages of using a third party distribution service company would appear to be:

> the ability to meet stringent customer service requirements at acceptable cost;
> reduction in the amount of capital employed in distribution;
> flexibility of capacity;
> increased geographical coverage;
> lower operating costs both overall and in peripheral areas;
> industrial relations risk-spreading;
> specialist services available, e.g. stock management;
> ability to redeploy management resources, and;
> overall risk reduction.

On the other hand there can be a number of disadvantages to set against the benefits:

> loss of direct control;
> inadequate performance feedback;
> stock rotation/product control reduced;
> possible loss of control on customer service;
> inability to respond to special demands;
> higher direct costs, and;
> communications problems with customers.

Many companies are now asking the question 'What business are we in?' and in some cases coming to the conclusion that their skills lie in manufacturing and marketing rather than in running a distribution system. In some cases this has led companies like Whitbreads, one of the UK's leading brewers, to set up a separate distribution company in partnership with a specialist third party operator, in this case the National Freight Corporation. Other companies have established distribution as a profit centre within their own business. This has the advantage of making distribution 'stand on its own feet' and enables the true costs and revenue potential of the distribution function to be identified. The four essential criteria for a profit centre are:

It employs capital.
It incurs cost.
It adds value.
It sets price.

Distribution meets the first three of these and, if it is given commercial freedom, it can set the price of the service that it provides. Many companies who have done this have also encouraged the profit centre to seek business elsewhere and a profitable business in its own right can result.

Consolidation and postponement

The concepts of consolidation and postponement in logistics whilst related may be considered separately.

Consolidation refers to the process of grouping together inventory, orders or shipments to gain greater cost economies. In a very real sense the benefits of the specialist distribution operator previously referred to came about through its ability to consolidate individual client company's movement and storage requirements. The same principles can also be applied within an individual company.

Benefits from inventory consolidation can be achieved by reducing the number of stock locations in the logistics system. There is a direct relationship between this and the total investment in inventory. By centralising inventory at a limited number of locations the same level of stock availability can be provided with less inventory. The reason for this is that each stock location could be regarded as serving its own market. That market will be subject to variation in daily demand which means that to provide an adequate service level safety stock will have to be carried in addition to the cycle stock necessary to meet expected demand. By consolidating stock at a more limited number of locations individual variation in individual market demand patterns can be subsumed within the total market variation. Put very simply, if a company has a warehouse at Bristol and another in Newcastle it is quite possible to find that local demand at Bristol leads to an out-of-stock situation on an item there, whilst there could be an overstock on the same product at Newcastle. By combining these two warehouses these situations can be balanced.

The actual reduction in the amount of inventory necessary to provide the same service if stock locations are consolidated seems to follow the 'square root rule'.[5] This states that the total inventory in a system is proportional to the square root of the number of locations at which a product is stocked. Thus a reduction from, say, 9 to 4 depots would result in a stock reduction of approximately one-third (i.e. from $\sqrt{9}$ to $\sqrt{4}$). The savings achievable by consolidation of stock location are shown in Table 2.1. Entries in this table are the percentage reductions in inventory when an N location system is changed to an M location system.

Table 2.1
Savings achievable by consolidation of inventory

N \ M	1	2	3	4	5	10	15
1							
2	29						
3	43	18					
4	50	29	13				
5	55	38	23	11			
10	68	55	45	38	29		
15	74	63	55	48	42	18	
20	78	68	61	55	50	29	13

Source: Maister.[5]

Consolidation as a concept can also be extended to transport. Here the aim is to maximise the utilisation of vehicles or to gain advantage of the lower unit costs when shipping larger consignments. Such consolidation can be achieved by grouping orders for a specific geographic market and by developing scheduled delivery programmes. This can be achieved by a better management of the order processing system so that as orders are received into the system their shipment can be planned in advance (see Chapter 6).

It may appear that both the consolidation of stockholding and the consolidation of shipments will lead to a deterioration in customer service by extending lead-times. This need not be so if the distribution system is run on the basis of planned deliveries rather than, as is so often the case, on the basis of reaction to customer orders as they arrive.

The concept of 'postponement' can provide a powerful means of improving logistics productivity if it is applied strategically. Bowersox[6] has defined postponement as a 'dimension of the sequence, timing and scale of operation necessary to support differentiated marketing. At the root of postponement is the economic principle of substitutability. In brief the two notions of postponement are: (1) postpone changes in form and identity to the latest possible point in the distribution system; and (2) postpone changes in inventory location to the latest possible point in time.'

The principle of postponement means that substantial savings in inventory can be gained by delaying as long as possible the transformation of a standard product into the specific version demanded by the customer. Thus a fertiliser manufacturer is currently investigating the possibility of mixing precise formulations from basic ingredients and bagging the final product all at the point of sale, rather than as is the case at present mixing and bagging at the plant. In a similar fashion ICI Paints has developed a paint mixing device for use with spray paint for cars which is installed at local distributors' premises. Thus from a very limited range of basic primary colours the local distributor can mix literally tens of thousands of colours to meet the specific requirements of local car body repair shops. Since there are such a vast number of car colours and since each repair job might only need a litre or two of paint it can be imagined that the cost of holding the paint in inventory in the form of final colours would be prohibitive.

This principle of postponement can be extended right through the operations of the company forcing us to think about radical changes in the way we manufacture and distribute our products. The introduction of flexible manufacturing systems (FMS) in many areas of industry will enable many more innovations along the lines of previous examples to become reality.

Summary

This chapter has explored the various impacts that logistics can have on corporate performance. The effects of logistics decisions can be widespread influencing the shape of both the profit and loss account and the balance sheet. The effective management of the logistics task can also improve cash flow as well as reduce working capital requirements. Finally by bringing logistics into the wider arena of corporate strategy many opportunities for strengthened market position can be grasped through new initiatives in customer service.

Notes

1   'Foremost-McKesson: The Computer moves Distribution to Center Stage' in *Business Week*, 7 December 1981.
2   *Perspectives on Experience*, Boston Consulting Group, 1968.
3   W. F. Friedman, 'Physical Distribution: The Concept of Shared Services' in *Harvard Business Review*, March/April 1975.
4   M. Christopher *et al.*, *Effective Distribution Management*, Pan Books, 1983.
5   D. H. Maister, 'Centralisation of Inventories and the "Square Root Law"' in *International Journal of Physical Distribution and Materials Management*, vol. 6, no. 3, 1975.
6   D. J. Bowersox, 'Emerging from the Recession: The Role of the Distribution Manager' in *Focus*, vol. 1, no. 2, July/August 1982.

3 Customer service and marketing

Although considerable managerial attention has been given recently to the improvement of marketing skills in the business, this has generally been limited to product, pricing and promotional strategy. Few companies have gone beyond a token espousal of the 'right product in the right place at the right time' to examine the marketing impact that cost-effective customer service policies can achieve. Part of the problem lies in the definition, and indeed the measurement, of customer service. In fact customer service has many dimensions and every business should understand that for each market segment in which they compete a specific service policy will need to be identified.

It is sometimes suggested that the role of logistics is to provide 'time and place utility' in the transfer of goods and services between buyer and seller. In other words there is no value in a product or service until it is in the hands of the customer or consumer. It follows that making the product or service 'available' is what the logistics function of the business is all about. 'Availability' is a complex concept, influenced by a galaxy of factors which together constitute customer service. These factors might include delivery frequency and reliability, stock levels and order cycle time, for example, as they are all affected by availability. Customer service is determined by the interaction of all those factors that affect the process of making products and services available to the buyer.

Definition of customer service

Many companies have varying views of customer service. LaLonde and Zinszer, in a study of customer service practices, found that in the industries they surveyed a range of views existed as to the definition of 'customer service':

All the activities required to accept, process, deliver and bill customer orders and to follow up on any activity that erred.

Timeliness and reliability of getting materials to customers in accordance with the customer's expectation.

A complex of activities involving all areas of the business which combine to deliver and invoice the company's products in a fashion that is perceived as satisfactory by the customer and which advances our company's objectives.

Total order entry, all communications with customers, all shipping, all freight, all invoicing and total control of repair of products.

Timely and accurate delivery of products ordered by customers with accurate follow-up and inquiry response including timely delivery of invoice.[1]

All these definitions are concerned with relationships at the buyer/seller interface. This same study suggested that customer service could be examined under three headings: pre-transaction elements; transaction elements, and post-transaction elements.

The pre-transaction elements of customer service relate to corporate policies or programmes, e.g. written statements of service policy, adequacy of organisational structure and system flexibility. The transaction elements are those variables directly involved in performing the physical distribution function, e.g. product availability, order cycle time, order status information and delivery reliability. The post-transaction elements are generally supportive of the product while in use, e.g. product warranty, parts and repair service, procedures for customer complaints and product replacement.

Many commentators have defined elements of customer service (e.g. Stephenson and Willett,[2] Christopher, Schary and Skjott-Larsen[3]) but the most common are as follows:

Order cycle time
Consistency and reliability of delivery
Inventory availability
Order-size constraints
Ordering convenience
Delivery times and flexibility
Invoicing procedures and accuracy

Claims procedure
Condition of goods on arrival
Salesmen's visits
Order status information.

In any particular product/market situation some of these elements will be more important than others and there may be other factors which have a significance in a specific market. Indeed it is essential to understand customer service in terms of the requirements of different market segments and that no universally appropriate list of elements exist; each market that the company serves will attach importance to different service elements.

Development of company policy

Because of the multivariate nature of customer service and the differing requirements of specific markets it is essential for any business to have a clearly identified policy towards customer service. It is perhaps surprising that so few companies have a defined policy, let alone the flexibility to manage and control it, when it is considered that service can be the most important element in the company's marketing mix. Considerable evidence exists to support the view that if a product is not available at the time the customer requires it, and a close substitute is available, then the sale will be lost to the competition. Even in markets where brand loyalty is strong a stockout might be sufficient to trigger off brand switching.[4,5] In industrial markets, too, the same pressures on purchasing source loyalty seem to be at work. Perrault and Russ[6] surveyed industrial purchasing officers using examples of standardised products and found that distribution service was considered second in importance only to product quality as a deciding criterion for vendor selection. Moreover, more than one-third of these purchasing officers indicated that they would cancel the order if it were not available for shipment when ordered. These findings were further reinforced in a study by Cunningham and Roberts.[7] Their investigation of the valve and pump manufacturing industry evaluated the service provided by suppliers of steel castings and forgings. Delivery reliability emerged as the primary element influencing the choice of supplier.

In the light of this and other evidence it is suggested that there are three basic requirements for the management of customer service:

1 Define an overall company philosophy of customer service in terms of attitude, organisation and responsibilities.
2 Develop internal standards for customer service, based on careful studies that have explored the quantitative trade-offs between various levels of customer service and the costs of achieving such levels, so as to identify the most profitable policy for each customer segment.
3 Inform customers what they might expect by way of customer service (perhaps in more general terms than the company defines its policies internally).[8]

To achieve the most effective deployment of corporate resources in developing a customer service policy along these lines the following prerequisites exist:

The perceptions of the parties to the purchasing decision in terms of customer service must be recognised.
The trade-off potential between the various components of the customer service mix must be evaluated.
The unique customer service requirement of each product/channel/market segment must be identified.

If cost-effective customer service policies are to be successfully developed and implemented within the firm, it is imperative that a formalised logic is adopted and closely followed (see figure 3.1). Customer service is too important and too costly to be left to chance. Thus the following six-step process is proposed:

Step 1: Identifying the key components of customer service

It is a common fault in marketing to fail to realise that customers do not always attach the same importance to product attributes as the vendor. Thus it sometimes happens that products are promoted on attributes or features that are less important to the customer in reality than other aspects. For example, a floor cleaner that is sold on its ease of application will not succeed unless 'ease of application' is a salient benefit sought by the customer. If 'shine' or the need for less frequent cleaning are more important to the customer then it might be better to feature those aspects in promotion. The same principle applies in customer service. Which aspects of service are rated most highly by the customer? If a company places its emphasis upon stock availability, but the customer regards delivery reliability more highly, it may not be allocating its resources in a way likely to maximise sales.

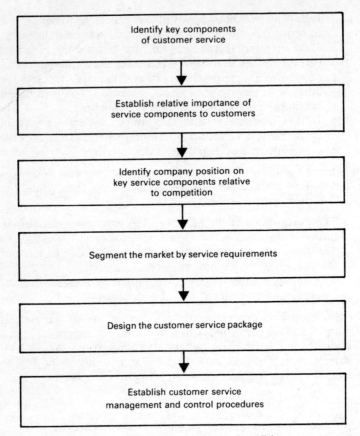

Figure 3.1   A framework for developing customer service policies

Alternatively a company that realises that its customers place a higher value on completeness of orders than they do on, say, regular scheduled deliveries could develop this to its advantage.

   Therefore it is important to gain an insight into the factors that influence buyer behaviour and, in the context of customer service, which particular elements are seen by the customer to be the most important.

Market research techniques

The use of market research techniques in distribution has lagged behind their application in such areas as product testing and advertising research, yet the importance of researching the service needs of customers is just as great as, say, the need to understand the market reaction to price. In fact it is possible to apply standard, proven market research methods to gain considerable insight into the ways that customers will react to customer service.

The first step in research of this type is to identify the relative source of influence upon the purchase decision. If, for example, we are selling components to a manufacturer, who will make the decision on the source of supply? This is not always an easy question to answer as in many cases there will be several people involved. The purchasing manager of the company to whom we are selling may only be acting as an agent for others within the firm. In other cases his influence will be much greater. Alternatively if we are manufacturing products for sale through retail outlets, is the decision to stock made centrally by a retail chain or by individual store managers? The answers can often be supplied by the sales force. The sales representative should know from experience who are the decision makers.

Given that a clear indication of the source of decision-making power can be gained the customer service researcher at least knows who to research. The question remains as to which elements of the vendor's total marketing offering have what effect upon the purchase decision.

Ideally once the decision-making unit in a specific market has been identified an initial, small-scale research programme should be initiated based upon personal interviews with a representative sample of buyers. The purpose of these interviews is to elicit, in the language of the customers, firstly the importance they attach to customer service vis-á-vis the other marketing mix elements such as price, product quality, promotion etc. and secondly, the specific importance they attach to the individual components of customer service.

There are various 'elicitation techniques' which can be used to draw from the respondents their views on these issues. One such technique that has been successfully used is the Kelly repertory grid, named after a North American psychologist, G. A. Kelly.[9] The technique is fairly straightforward to administer. The usual procedure is to prepare a set of cards on each of which is written the name of a competing company in the product/market area under investigation. The respondent is asked to go through the cards and discard any company names with which they are not familiar. Three cards are then selected at random from the pack and the respondent is asked to consider the names of the companies shown on the cards and to answer the question: 'Which two of these three suppliers are more similar in terms of the service they provide than the third, and why?' With only a little prompting the respondent can usually produce two or three reasons. For example: 'These two are more reliable on deliveries than this one'; 'These two have better informed sales representatives'; 'This one tends to deliver fewer part orders'.

Already the respondent has provided us with three criteria that he/she uses when evaluating suppliers: delivery reliability; information from sales representatives and completeness of orders.

A further random triad of cards is then presented to the respondent and the same question asked. Perhaps this time additional dimensions will emerge; for example, quality of packaging and policy on returned goods. The process is continued until no further new elements of service are revealed. By repeating this procedure with further individuals it is possible to identify those dimensions which occur most commonly. There are more sophisticated ways of reducing this initial list of customer service elements into a number of underlying dimensions using factor analysis,[10] but for most purposes in this research it is only necessary to interview about a dozen respondents to see a pattern of responses emerging. The author was recently involved in a customer service study that used the repertory grid technique to determine the elements of customer service in the market for a particular grocery product and an initial series of personal interviews were conducted with senior buyers responsible for the purchase of that product in major retail outlets. As a result 23 customer service elements were generated, of which six occurred most often, as follows:

> Frequency of delivery
> Time from order to delivery*
> Reliability of delivery*
> Emergency deliveries when required
> Stock availability and continuity of supply*
> Orders filled completely
> Advice on non-availability*
> Convenience of placing order
> Acknowledgement of order
> Accuracy of invoices
> Quality of sales representation*
> In-store merchandising support*
> Regular calls by sales representatives
> Manufacturer monitoring of retail stock levels
> Credit terms offered

Customer query handling
Quality of outer packaging
Well-stacked pallets
Easy-to-read use-by dates on outers
Quality of inner package for in-store handling and display
Consults on new product/package development
Reviews product range regularly
Co-ordination between production, distribution and
    marketing
(*Items occurring most often)

An alternative approach to the generation of the service elements relevant to a specific market segment is the group interview. Levy describes a study of wholesalers in the pharmaceutical industry where seven senior managers from major wholesalers were brought together as a group.[11] Using the nominal group technique he generated sixty-six elements of customer service relevant to that sector of the industry. The process is in four stages. First, the group is asked to generate ideas silently. Second, the ideas are recorded in a round-robin fashion. The third stage consists of a discussion of each idea. Finally the group votes on each item's importance.

Whatever technique is used the importance of this initial step in developing a customer service policy is that relevant and meaningful measures of customer service are generated by the customers themselves. Once these dimensions are defined we can identify the relative importance of each one and the extent to which the customer is prepared to trade-off one aspect of service for another.

Step 2: Establishing the relative importance of customer service components

It has been shown that the supplier's view of what is important, as far as customer service is concerned, may differ from the views of the customer. In a study by Marr[12] differences were identified in the importance attached by buyers and sellers to aspects of customer service in a particular industry. Often the customer may form an opinion of the service provided by a particular supplier on the basis of a relationship built up over a period of time rather than on any 'hard', measurable criteria such as order cycle time or shortages. It is important to recognise that customer service is essentially about perceptions, which will be influenced by a combination of experience, buyer–seller relationships and beliefs about alternative sources of supply.

One of the simplest ways of discovering the importance a customer attaches to customer service would be to take the components generated by means of the process described in Step 1 and to ask a representative sample of customers to rank order them from the 'most important' to the 'least important'. In practice this would be difficult, particularly with a large number of components, and would not give any insight into the relative importance of each element. Alternatively a form of rating scale could be used. For example, the respondents could be asked to place a weight from 1 to 10 against each component according to how much importance they attached to each element. The problem here is that respondents will tend to rate most of the components as highly important, especially since those components were generated on the grounds of salience anyway. A partial solution is to ask the respondent to allocate a total of 100 points amongst all the elements listed, according to perceived importance. However, this is a fairly daunting task for the respondent and can often result in an arbitrary allocation.

Trade-off techniques

Fortunately a relatively recent innovation in consumer research technology now enables us to evaluate very simply the implicit importance that a customer attaches to the separate elements of customer service. The technique is based around the concept of trade-off and can best be illustrated by an example from everyday life. In considering, say, the purchase of a new car we might seek specific attributes, e.g. performance in terms of speed and acceleration, economy in terms of petrol consumption, size in terms of passenger and luggage capacity and, of course, low price. However, it is unlikely that any one car will meet all of these requirements so we are forced to trade-off one or more attributes against the others.

The same is true of the customer faced with alternative options of distribution service. He might be prepared to sacrifice a day or two on lead-time in order to gain delivery reliability, or to trade-off order completeness against improvements in order entry etc. Perrault and Russ[13] were amongst the first to report on the application of trade-off analysis to physical distribution service. More recently Levy[14] summarised further applications of the technique to the customer service problem. Essentially the technique works by presenting the respondent with feasible combinations of customer service elements and asking for a rank order or preference for those combinations.

Let us take a simple example where a respondent is asked to choose between different levels of stock availability, order cycle time and delivery reliability. For the sake of example the following options are presented:

Stock availability – 75 per cent
                     – 85 per cent
                     – 95 per cent
Order cycle time   – 2 days
                     – 3 days
                     – 4 days
Delivery reliability– ± 1 day
                     – ± 3 days

The various trade-offs can be placed before the respondent as a series of matrices:

Order cycle time

		2 days	3 days	4 days
	75%			9
Stock availability	85%			
	95%	1		

Order cycle time

		2 days	3 days	4 days
Delivery reliability	±1 day	1		
	±3 days			6

Stock availability

		75%	85%	95%
Delivery reliability	±1 day			1
	±3 days	6		

The idea is that the respondent should complete each matrix to illustrate his/her preference for service alternatives. Thus with the first trade-off matrix between order cycle time and stock availability it is presumed that the most preferred combination would be an order cycle time of 2 days with a stock availability of 95 per cent and the least preferred combination an order cycle time of 5 days with a stock availability of 75 per cent. But what about the other combinations? Here the respondent is asked to complete the matrix to show his own preference. An example of a typical response is given below:

Order cycle time

		2 days	3 days	4 days
	75%	6	8	9
Stock availability	85%	3	5	7
	95%	1	2	4

Order cycle time

		2 days	3 days	4 days
Delivery reliability	±1 day	1	3	5
	±3 days	2	4	6

Stock availability

		75%	85%	95%
Delivery reliability	±1 day	4	2	1
	±3 days	6	5	3

Using a computer programme based upon Johnson's non-metric trade-off procedure[15] the implicit 'importance weights' that underlie the initial preference rankings can be generated. For the data in the above example the following weights emerge:

Service element		*Importance weight*
1 Stock availability	75 per cent	− 0.480
	85 per cent	0
	95 per cent	+ 0.480
2 Delivery time	2 days	+ 0.456
	3 days	0
	4 days	− 0.456
3 Delivery reliability	± 1 day	+ 0.239
	± 3 days	− 0.239

Thus for this respondent stock availability would appear to be marginally more important than delivery time and both were in the region of twice as important as delivery reliability. When later we come to discuss the concept of a 'service package' information such as this can be most useful. It can tell us for example that, in this hypothetical case, a stock availability of 85 per cent with 2 days' delivery and a reliability of ± 1 day is seen as being equally acceptable as a 95 per cent availability with 2 days' delivery and ± 3 days' reliability (a combined weight of 0.695 compared with 0.697). Thus suggesting that a tightening up on reliability might reduce stockholding and still provide an acceptable level of customer service.

A further benefit of this type of information is that it enables us to define the responses between types of customers – a most important consideration when examining the possibilities of differentiating the service offering by market segment.

The particular version of trade-off analysis described above suffers from one shortcoming, i.e. it presents only a series of pairwise comparisons one at a time rather than complete service packages which, it could be argued, is more realistic. An alternative method which overcomes this problem, but adds to the complexity of the respondent task, is conjoint analysis using the MONANOVA computer program developed by Kruskal and Carmone.[16] An application of this approach to customer service is described by Christopher et al.[17]

Whatever method is used the benefit of this approach is that it enables data to be collected relatively easily, in the form of rank order preferences, and converts it into highly useful information about the real importance customers attach to different components of the total service offering.

Step 3: Identifying company position on key components of service

Now we know from the previous two steps the key components of customer service and their relative importance the next question is: 'How do my customers rate me on these components compared with the competition?'

The first two steps were accomplished using relatively small samples and in effect they served as a 'pilot' study to provide the basis for a larger scale survey of the company's customers. This can often be achieved by means of a postal questionnaire, the sample for which is chosen to reflect the different types of customer.

The main purpose of the questionnaire is to present the components of service as elicited in Step 1 and to ask the respondents to rate the company and its competitors on each of these elements in terms of their perceived performance. Table 3.1 reproduces part of the questionnaire that was used in the grocery products study referred to above. For each competing company in that market the respondent was asked to rate its performance on each of the 23 relevant dimensions of service identified in Step 1. When the responses were aggregated by trade sector clear patterns emerged. On each customer service element it was possible to see how each competing supplier compared in terms of each other, and to identify relative performance on those aspects of service that had been identified in the previous Steps as having greater importance.

Other analyses can include regional breakdowns and analyses by size and type of customer. The usual statistical tests can be applied to identify if different scores on any dimensions have significance. To ensure an unbiased response to the questionnaire it is preferable if the survey can be carried out anonymously or via a third party such as a market research agency. Also, as in Steps 1 and 2, it is important to make sure that the people to whom the questionnaire is sent represent the decision-making structure within their concerns.

Management now has a customer service data base upon which it can make a number of crucial decisions regarding the design of more cost-effective customer service policies.

Step 4: Segmenting the market by service requirements

Many companies recognise the considerable advantages in not treating markets as if they were homogeneous, with customers

Table 3.1
Customer service questionnaire (part)

How would you rate X Y Z on the following: (Score from 1 to 5; 1 = very poor, 5 = excellent)	Please circle
Frequency of delivery	1 2 3 4 5
Time from order to delivery	1 2 3 4 5
Reliability of delivery	1 2 3 4 5
Emergency deliveries when required	1 2 3 4 5
Stock availability and continuity of supply	1 2 3 4 5
Orders filled completely	1 2 3 4 5
Advice on non-availability	1 2 3 4 5
Convenience of placing order	1 2 3 4 5
Acknowledgement of order	1 2 3 4 5
Accuracy of invoices	1 2 3 4 5
Quality of sales representation	1 2 3 4 5
Regular calls by sales reps	1 2 3 4 5
In-store merchandising support	1 2 3 4 5
Manufacturer monitoring of retail stock levels	1 2 3 4 5
Credit terms offered	1 2 3 4 5
Customer query handling	1 2 3 4 5
Quality of outer packaging	1 2 3 4 5
Well-stacked pallets	1 2 3 4 5
Easy-to-read use-by dates on outers	1 2 3 4 5
Quality of inner package for in-store handling and display	1 2 3 4 5
Consults on new product/package development	1 2 3 4 5
Reviews product range regularly	1 2 3 4 5
Co-ordination between production, distribution and marketing	1 2 3 4 5

sharing common characteristics and seeking similar benefits from the products or services on offer. Those companies realise that within a total market there will normally be a number of distinct sub-markets or segments each with distinct characteristics or requirements. Sometimes these differences can be catered for by a strategy of product differentiation, that is adjusting the nature of the product or service to meet the specific needs of a segment. However, it may also be possible to target the product or service more specifically at chosen market segments by varying other elements of the marketing mix such as price, promotion or, in this case, customer service.

The questions to be asked are:

Do all our customers require the same level of service?
Are all our customers equally sensitive to service?
What are the different requirements of different market segments, or trade sectors, for customer service?

The underlying philosophy is that it is insufficient to offer a blanket level of service across all market segments or trade sectors. It may be that for some segments the service offered is higher than necessary to achieve the sale and for other segments it may be too low. Equally some segments may respond more to one aspect of service than another. To develop cost-effective customer service policies it is necessary to recognise these important differences between customer segments. Whilst it is not suggested that every customer's particular requirement should be specifically catered for, it is important to attempt to isolate major groupings in the total market and to recognise the service factors which have the greatest impact on them.

Examples of segmentation studies

Only a limited number of customer service segmentation studies have been reported in the literature. One such study by Gilmour et al.[18] looked at the scientific instrument industry and found that a number of different segments did exist with different service requirements. For example, private companies viewed delivery time and telephone order handling as more important and after sales service as less important than other segments in the market. Government departments on the other hand, the study showed, consider after-sales service to be more important. Secondary schools valued ordering convenience the highest.

Other studies, conducted amongst shoppers, have shown that differences exist in the reactions of customers to out-of-stock situations. A study by Neilsen in the USA[19] and by Schary and Christopher in the UK[20] revealed that there were noticeable differences in subsequent behaviour when the shopper was faced with a stock-out of the preferred brand. For example, the UK study revealed different responses between those shoppers naming the store's own label as the preferred brand as against a manufacturer's branded item (see table 3.2).

Companies now recognise that markets are becoming increasingly sensitive to service and that 'availability' can overcome brand loyalty – if the preferred brand is not available but a competitor's is, the sale will switch. But availability is just one dimension of service, albeit the crucial one to the end user. At the trade level reliability might be rated more highly amongst some buyers, or condition of goods on arrival. The purpose of market segmentation when applied to customer service is to establish these differences and to derive strategies to capitalise upon them.

Table 3.2
Action taken by shoppers following stock-out

	Store's own label %	Other brand %
Purchased same brand, different size	8.5	3.4
Bought other brand	12.0	10.3
Bought other product	12.8	12.0
Postponed purchase	22.6	8.5
Decided not to purchase	23.9	7.7
Decided to search in other store	20.5	66.2
	100.0	100.0

Cluster analysis techniques

How can these customer service segments be identified? One technique that has been successfully used is cluster analysis.[21] It is conceptually simple although computer analysis is usually necessary. It could be used directly on the results emerging from Step 2. Thus for each of the elements of customer service there will be an importance weight ascribed by each respondent. This information can be arrayed in the form of a matrix as shown in table 3.3.

In each column of the matrix would be the importance weight attributed by each respondent to each service element. The cluster analysis routine then seeks out those respondents who are most similar to each other in terms of their scores on all the elements. In other words groups with matching scores are identified. There may well emerge a number of distinct groups the members of which exhibit similar responses within the group but are different from members of the other groups.

Whilst this information may reveal many insights it is only of real value if there are operational differences between the groups. Let us say, for example, that one group to emerge from the cluster analysis was found on examination to comprise mainly discount stores whilst another group comprised cash and carry wholesalers. In such a situation it is possible to think in terms of developing differential service policies to meet the needs of these different categories of outlet.

Table 3.3
Basic input data for cluster analysis

	Respondents				
	1	2	3	— — — — — —	n
Customer service elements					
Frequency of delivery					
Time from order to delivery					
Reliability of delivery					
"					
"					
"					
"					
"					
"					
"					
Co-ordination between pro-duction and marketing					

Even without the use of cluster analysis it is often possible to identify major groupings simply by comparing 'profiles' derived from the responses given to the questionnaire described in Step 3. The most important thing is the recognition that different customer types may have different customer service requirements and that it is rarely likely to be cost-effective to offer the same customer service package across the whole market. This is the message of market segmentation.

Step 5: Designing the customer service package

To compete effectively in any market requires the ability to develop some differential advantage over competing companies and their product or service offerings. This advantage may be in terms of distinctive product attributes or related benefits as perceived by the customer. It may be price or alternatively the product may be promoted in such a way that it acquires a distinctive image in the eyes of the market. In just the same way customer service can be used to develop a differential advantage which is of benefit to the company. For example, in competitive markets where real product differentiation may be difficult to establish and where competition on price would only lead to profit erosion, it makes sense to switch the marketing emphasis to customer service.

The current battle in the office copier market provides a case in point. Xerox, the early leader in this field, has found that competition has become increasingly severe from products which, to the potential customer at least, seem to offer the same product benefits. Pressure on margins is considerable and price cutting would not provide a lasting solution for Xerox. Instead it has switched the emphasis to service. Its recent advertisements underline this point:

> 'Because the best way to get new customers is to keep your current ones happy, Xerox offers the largest service force in the business – over 30,000 men and women worldwide.

> Parts inventories and parts distribution systems are all part of our job. That's why we have distribution centres around the globe.

> So, chances are, our technical representatives will always have what you need where you need it. Whenever possible, we standardise parts so that they're interchangeable from country to country. That way we can take better care of our copiers and our customers.'

Similar approaches have been used by companies such as Digital Equipment Corporation and Caterpillar who have built up commanding positions in their markets and maintained them through the effective use of customer service.

The theme of this chapter has been the need to establish those components of the total customer service mix which have the greatest impact on the buyer's perception of us as a supplier. This thinking needs to be carried right through into the design of the customer service offering or 'package', for it will most likely contain more than one component.

The design of the package will need to take account of the different market segments so that the resources allocated to customer service can be used in the most cost-effective way. Too often a uniform, blanket approach to service is adopted by companies which does not distingusih between the real requirements of different customer types. This can lead to customers either being offered too little service or too much.[22]

Several authors have suggested ways in which competitive service packages might be designed.[23,24] In a recent presentation Shycon and Ritz[25] described one approach to the development of such a package which contained the following steps:

–   Determining competitive customer service practices and policies within each product and market channel.
–   Identifying and measuring key elements which led to becoming a preferred, or 'most favoured supplier'.
–   Measuring the impact of each aspect of service on market share and profitability.
–   Assessing the performance of the company on each of these service components.
–   Redesigning the corporate service package to emphasise effective service expenditures and de-emphasise ineffective ones.

They identified in a study of one firm's customers, that sensitivity to different service elements varied considerably by market channel, geographic area and product category. More importantly they isolated two distinct effects of different service levels: firstly a short-term effect on sales, and secondly a long-term effect on achieving a more favoured position with the buyer. For this particular company selling to a specific market segment they were able to suggest an improved service package designed to influence the purchasing decision maker in order to achieve a more favoured long-term position. Recommendations for the redesigned service package included:

1   In designing the distribution system consider the added buyer influence and the impact on sales of a 'market presence', i.e. proximity of stock to key markets.
2   Provide quantity price brackets, encouraging the buyer to 'stretch' for a lower price through purchasing greater quantities – especially at the lowest quantity levels.
3   Offer promotion incentives, especially to lower volume customers.

4   Support promotions with superior distribution service.
5   Provide incentives to reduce 'customer responsible' emergency shipment needs.
6   Concentrate on improved on-time delivery consistency.
7   Recognise the influence of sales and service personnel on sales levels achieved.

The precise composition of the customer service package for any market segment will depend upon the results of the analysis described in the previous steps. It will also be determined by budgetary and cost constraints and this is where the trade-off analysis previously described can be helpful. If alternative packages can be identified which seem to be equally acceptable to the buyer it makes sense to choose the least cost alternative. For example it may be possible to identify a customer service package with high acceptability which enables the emphasis to be switched away from a high level of inventory availability towards, say, improved customer communication.

Once a cost-effective package has been identified in this way it should become a major part of the company's marketing mix: 'using service to sell' is the message here. If the market segments are sensitive to service then the service package must be actively promoted. One way to achieve this with great effect is to stress the impact on the *customer's* costs of the improved service package, e.g. what improved reliability will do for his own stock planning, what shorter lead times will do for his inventory levels, how improved ordering and invoicing systems will lead to fewer errors etc. All too often the customer will not appreciate the impact that improved service offered by the supplier can have on his own bottom line.

Beyond the simple presentation of a marketing message based around an improved customer service package lies the opportunity to develop tailor-made service offerings, particularly to key accounts, based upon 'negotiated' service levels. The idea here is that no two customers are alike, either in terms of their requirements or, specifically, in terms of their profitability to the supplier. One UK-based company in the consumer electronics field identified that whilst three of its major customers were roughly equivalent in terms of their annual sales value there were considerable differences in the costs generated by each. For example, one customer required delivery to each of its 300 plus retail outlets, whilst the others took delivery at one central warehouse. Similarly one company paid within 30 days of receiving the invoice; the others took nearer to 40 days to pay.

Again, one of the three was found to place twice as many 'emergency' orders as the others. Careful analysis of the true costs showed that the profitability of the three customers differed by over 20 per cent. Yet each customer received the same value-related discounts and the same level of customer service.

Conducting such a 'customer account profitability' analysis can provide the supplier with not only the basis on which to negotiate price but also a basis for 'negotiating' service. Whilst companies in the United States tend to be familiar with the importance of relating price discounts to customer related costs, because of Robinson-Patman legislation, it is rarely used elsewhere in a positive way. Thus whilst the concept of paying more for an airmail letter than a surface letter is well established, say, it is less common to find a supplier offering different 'qualities' of service at different prices. Interestingly enough the business manager who accepts the difference between first class, business class and tourist class on the plane he takes to see his customer might never think of how that same principle could be applied to his own business.

Step 6: Establishing customer service management and control procedures

It is one thing to follow the logic implied in the sequential process outlined so far. It is something else however to implement the resulting policy and control it. Most of the available evidence suggests that companies do not have a defined policy towards customer service in the first place. Even those companies that do lay down a policy towards customer service rarely do so in terms of hard, quantifiable service standards that can be measured and reported on as part of a continuing control process.

It is essential that customer service goals are based upon the strategic objectives of the company as a whole, and that the development of a customer service policy can only take place as part of a global review of the company's marketing strategy. However, within this strategy customer service has its own particular role which could be described as: 'getting product to customers at service levels that are equal to or better than the competitor's, and doing so at costs that permit competitive pricing and adequate profit contribution'.[26]

To achieve this aim, that is a customer service policy which is both cost-effective and consonant with wider corporate objectives, a systematic and formalised approach to customer service management is essential.

A prerequisite for customer-service oriented distribution management is an appropriate organisation structure. Customer service failings are often due to organisational problems. Frequently it is found that responsibility for the various elements of customer service, if they are managed at all, is spread around the organisation with little attempt at co-ordination between them.

For example, who determines policy on finished goods inventory levels? It is probably not the same person responsible for delivery times. Likewise, who handles customer queries? Probably not the department responsible for order entry. In other words the company ends up with a diversity of uncoordinated customer service activities which do not appear as a cohesive whole to the market.

The only way around this problem is through effective customer service management, which requires that all those activities involved from the time the order is placed until the goods are delivered are managed as an integrated function. Thus order processing, order status, order assembly, stock management, transport scheduling and even invoicing must ultimately be the responsibility of a specifically designated customer service function.

Some of the more forward-looking companies have recognised the need to introduce the customer service function as a means of coordinating marketing, distribution and production as they affect the customer. Customer service begins when the order is taken and to ensure the satisfactory delivery of that order to meet customer requirements a high degree of integration must be achieved within the supplier's business. The appointment of a 'customer service manager' as a progress chaser is not enough. Such a person would need to have authority to set priorities, to remedy bottlenecks and to coordinate the various activities involved from receipt of order through to delivery of goods. The customer service management function must also be involved in the determination of customer service policies. It is arguable that such a far-reaching function as this could not be managed by a single department. Indeed there is a case for making customer service a cross-functional concern to ensure the greatest commitment to agreed objectives by all the business functions concerned. The proper place for the day-to-day management of customer service would be in the logistics function rather than as a separate activity. There is no one prescription for the organisational positioning of customer service – different businesses will have different needs – but it is essential that the role of customer service management is recognised and implemented.

Notes

1   B. J. LaLonde and P. H. Zinszer, *Customer Service: Meaning & Measurement*, NCPDM, Chicago 1976.
2   P. R. Stephenson and R. P. Willett, 'Selling with Physical Distribution Service' in *Business Horizons*, December 1968.
3   M. G. Christopher, P. Schary and T. Skjott-Larsen, *Customer Service and Distribution Strategy*, Associated Business Press, 1979.
4   J. U. Farley, 'Why does Brand Loyalty Vary Over Products?' in *Journal of Marketing Research*, vol. 1, no. 1, 1964.
5   P. B. Schary and M. G. Christopher, 'The Anatomy of a Stock-Out' in *Journal of Retailing*, vol. 55, no. 2, Summer 1979.
6   W. D. Perrault and F. A. Russ, 'Physical Distribution Service in Industrial Purchase Decisions' in *Journal of Marketing*, vol. 40, April 1976.
7   M. T. Cunningham and D. A. Roberts, 'The Role of Customer Service in Industrial Marketing' in *European Journal of Marketing*, vol. 8, no. 1, 1974.
8   Adapted from D. P. Herron, 'Making Dollars and Sense out of Customer Service', Working Paper *SRI International*, 1982.
9   G. A. Kelly, *The Psychology of Personal Constructs*, Norton, 1955.
10 F. Fransella and D. Bannister, *A Manual for Repertory Grid Technique*, Academic Press, 1971.
11 M. Levy, 'Customer Service: A Managerial Approach to Controlling Marketing Channel Conflict' in *International Journal of Physical Distribution and Materials Management*, vol. 11, no. 7, 1981.
12 N. E. Marr, 'Do Managers Really Know What Service their Customers Require?' in *International Journal of Physical Distribution and Materials Management*, vol. 10, no. 7, 1980.
13 W. D. Perrault and F. A. Russ, 'Improving Physical Distribution Service Decisions with Trade-off Analysis' in *International Journal of Physical Distribution and Materials Management*, vol. 7, no. 3, 1977.
14 M. Levy, 'Diminishing Returns for Customer Service' in *International Journal of Physical Distribution and Materials Management*, vol. 11, no. 1, 1981.
15 R. M. Johnson, 'Beyond Conjoint Measurement: A Method of Pairwise Trade-off Analysis' in B. B. Anderson (ed.), *Advances in Consumer Research Proceedings*, vol. III, Sixth

Annual Conference, Association for Consumer Research, 1976.

16 J. B. Kruskal and F. J. Carmone, 'MONANOVA: A Fortran IV Program for Monotone Analysis of Variance' in *Behavioural Science*, vol. 14, April 1969.

17 M. G. Christopher, P. Schary and T. Skjott-Larsen, *op. cit.*

18 P. Gilmour *et al.*, 'Customer Service: Differentiating by Market Segment' in *International Journal of Physical Distribution*, vol. 7, no. 3, 1977.

19 'Growing Problems of Stock-outs Verified by Neilsen Research' in *Progressive Grocer*, November 1968.

20 P. B. Schary and M. G. Christopher, 'The Anatomy of a Stock-Out' in *Journal of Retailing*, vol. 55, no. 2, Summer 1979.

21 M. G. Christopher, 'Cluster Analysis & Market Segmentation' in *British Journal of Marketing*, vol. 3, no. 2, 1969.

22 R. E. Sabath, 'How Much Service Do Customers Really Want?' in *Business Horizons*, April 1978.

23 W. M. Hutchinson and J. F. Stolle, 'How to Manage Customer Service' in *Harvard Business Review*, vol. 46, no. 6, November/December 1968.

24 W. D. Perrault and F. A. Russ, 'Physical Distribution Service: A Neglected Aspect of Marketing Management' in *MSU Business Topics*, vol. 22, no. 3, 1974.

25 H. N. Shycon and C. J. Ritz, *Analytical Techniques to Evaluate Service Levels Required for Sales Growth and Profitability*, Shycon Associates Inc., Waltham, Mass 02154, USA.

26 W. Blanding, '12 Tips No Salesman Wants to Hear or can Afford to Live Without' in *Sales Management*, vol. 114, no. 3, 1975.

4   The costs of distribution

Probably one of the most important reasons why the adoption of an integrated approach to logistics and distribution management has proved so difficult for many companies is the lack of appropriate cost information. The need to manage the total distribution activity as a complete system, having regard for the effects of decisions taken in one cost area upon other cost areas, has implications for the cost accounting system of the firm. Typically, conventional accounting systems group costs into broad, aggregated categories which do not then allow the more detailed analysis necessary to identify the true costs of servicing customers with particular product mixes. Without this facility to analyse aggregated cost data it becomes impossible to reveal the potential for cost trade-offs that may exist within the logistics system.

The latter point is crucial as the concept of the cost trade-off lies at the heart of successful logistics management. The trade-off principle is based upon the notion that it is possible to make a change in one component of the logistics mix which may well increase the costs in that area but which will lead to an overall improvement in total costs and/or performance in the system as a whole. So, for example, a logistics system with five regional depots incurs higher warehouse and stockholding costs than a system with only one national distribution centre, but the savings in inventory carrying costs and the reduction in inter-depot movements under the latter system may more than compensate for any additional transport costs – or vice versa.

Generally, the effects of trade-offs are assessed in two ways: from the point of view of their impact on total system costs, and from their impact on sales revenue. It may be possible to trade off costs in such a way that total costs increase, yet because of the better service now being offered, sales revenue also increases. If the difference between revenue and costs is greater than before, the trade-off may be regarded as leading to an improvement in cost effectiveness. However, without an adequate logistics-oriented cost accounting system it is extremely difficult to identify the extent to which a particular trade-off is cost-beneficial.

The concept of total cost analysis

Many problems at the operational level in logistics management arise because all the impacts of specific decisions, both direct and indirect, throughout the corporate system are not taken into account. Too often decisions taken in one area can lead to unforeseen results in other areas. Changes in policy on minimum order value, for example, may influence customer ordering patterns and lead to additional costs. Similarly changes in production schedules with a view to improving production efficiency may lead to reductions in finished stock availability and thus affect customer service.

The problems associated with identifying the total system impact of distribution policies are immense. By its very nature logistics cuts across traditional company organisation functions with cost impacts on most of those functions. Conventional accounting systems do not usually assist in the identification of these company-wide impacts, frequently absorbing logistics-related costs in other cost elements. The cost of processing orders for example is an amalgam of specific costs incurred in different functional areas of the business which generally prove extremely difficult to bring together. Figure 4.1 outlines the various cost elements involved in the complete order processing cycle.

Accounting practice for budgeting and standard-setting has tended to result in a compartmentalisation of company accounts, thus budgets tend to be set on a functional basis and the accounting systems are similarly structured on a functional basis. The trouble is that policy costs do not unsually confine themselves within the same watertight boundaries. It is the nature of logistics that, like a stone thrown into a pond, the effects of policies spread beyond their immediate area of impact.

A further feature of logistics decisions contributing to the complexity of generating appropriate cost information is that they are usually taken against a background of an existing system. The purpose of total cost analysis in this context is to identify the

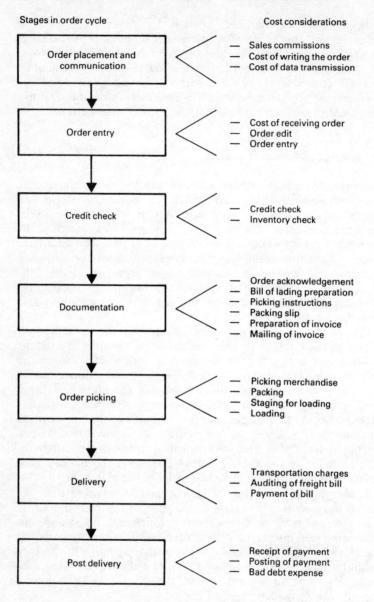

Stages in order cycle

Cost considerations

Order placement and communication
— Sales commissions
— Cost of writing the order
— Cost of data transmission

Order entry
— Cost of receiving order
— Order edit
— Order entry

Credit check
— Credit check
— Inventory check

Documentation
— Order acknowledgement
— Bill of lading preparation
— Picking instructions
— Packing slip
— Preparation of invoice
— Mailing of invoice

Order picking
— Picking merchandise
— Packing
— Staging for loading
— Loading

Delivery
— Transportation charges
— Auditing of freight bill
— Payment of bill

Post delivery
— Receipt of payment
— Posting of payment
— Bad debt expense

Source: D. M. Lambert, M. L. Bennion and J. C. Taylor, 'Solving the Small Order Problem' in *International Journal of Physical Distribution and Materials Management*, vol. 13, no. 1, 1983.

Figure 4.1   Stages and costs associated with an order

change in costs brought about by these decisions. The cost must therefore be viewed in incremental terms – the change in total costs caused by the change to the system. Thus the addition of an extra warehouse to the distribution network will bring about cost changes in transport, inventory investment and communications, e.g. order processing. It is the incremental cost difference which is the relevant accounting information for decision making in this case. Figure 4.2 shows how total logistics costs can be influenced by the addition, or removal, of a depot from the system.

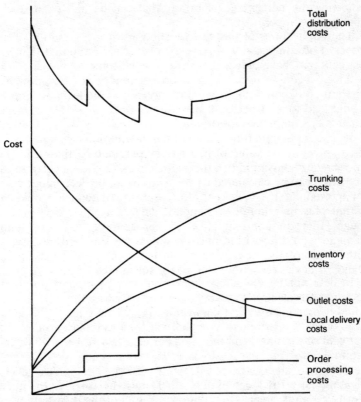

Figure 4.2 The total costs of a distribution network

It can be seen therefore that the logistics cost accounting problem is substantial and yet it must be solved for the full potential of improved logistics management to be realised.

The cost of providing customer service

In the discussion of customer service in Chapter 3 it was implicit that the provision of distribution service involves costs. Furthermore, the higher the level of service offered, the higher will be the costs. In fact it can be shown that once the level of service increases beyond the 70-80 per cent mark, the associated costs increase far more than proportionately ('service level' here reflecting the percentage of orders that can be met from stock within a given period).

The implications of this cost function are worth attention. The effect of offering, say, a 97 per cent level of service rather than 95 per cent may have only a slight effect on customer demand, yet it will have a considerable effect on distribution costs – for normally distributed demand this 2 per cent increase in the level of service would lead to a 14 per cent increase in safety stock. The reasons for this are simply demonstrated.

If sales of an item follow the normal distribution (see figure 4.3) then knowing the value of its two key parameters, the mean $(\bar{x})$ and standard deviation (σ), the probability of a given level of sales occurring can be calculated easily. Thus it can be determined that on approximately 68 per cent of occasions total demand would be within plus or minus one standard deviation either side of the mean; that on approximately 95 per cent of occasions total demand would lie within plus or minus two standard deviations either side of the mean and on 99 per cent of occasions three standard deviations either side of the mean (see figure 4.4).

In determining the safety stock necessary to support different required service levels we are concerned only with those occasions when demand is greater than average $(\bar{x})$. If the sales of this item are normally distributed, demand will be lower than average 50 per cent of the time, and thus a 50 per cent service level would be maintained from cycle stock alone (that quantity of stock necessary to meet expected demand). To provide service levels higher than 50 per cent safety stock must be carried. In other words, we must focus attention on the area of the distribution to the right of the mean. Thus by setting a stock level one standard deviation greater than the mean, a service level of approximately 84 per cent can be achieved. By setting the inventory level two standard deviations greater than the mean the service level is approximately 98 per cent and with three standard deviations it would be 99.9 per cent.

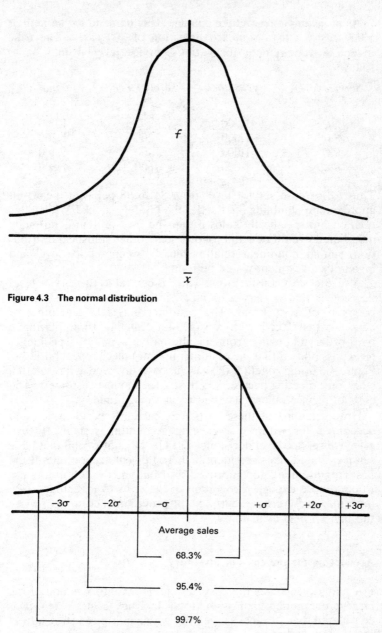

Figure 4.3 The normal distribution

Figure 4.4 Probability of level of sales being within given limits

As an example let us take average daily demand for an item as 1,000 cases with a standard deviation of 200 cases. The total inventory requirement for various service levels would be as follows:

Service level	Cycle stock	Safety stock	Total
%			
50	1,000	–	1,000
84	1,000	200	1,200
98	1,000	400	1,400
99.9	1,000	600	1,600

Thus to increase service level from 84 to 98 per cent means an approximate doubling in the level of safety stock. Whilst this relationship specifically holds if demand for the item is normally distributed even if demand follows some other statistical distribution, similar non-linear relationships between service level and inventory investment would be found.

A further cost consideration which is central to the service level decision is that of service failures, in particular the cost to the company of a stock-out. The customer may take a number of actions when faced with a stock-out, ranging from placing a back-order to buying from an alternative supplier. The longer term possibility is that the customer may not place repeat business. Figure 4.5 brings together the various costs involved as a result of a stock-out: meeting back orders, lost sales and lost customers. The costs of service failure may be of some magnitude.

However none of these costs may currently be identified and accounted for within the existing accounting system. If cost-effective service level decisions are to be taken it is vital that basic service-related costs are identified. In this connection one of the basic requirements for improved distribution cost accounting has to be a more explicit recognition of the costs of inventory, since inventory decisions are central to the provision of customer service through product availability.

Accounting for the costs of inventory

For many companies the cost of holding inventory is one of the largest components of their total logistics cost. When it is considered that a chain of inventory within a firm can stretch from raw materials through to finished goods and will encompass work in progress and goods in transit it will be appreciated just how high

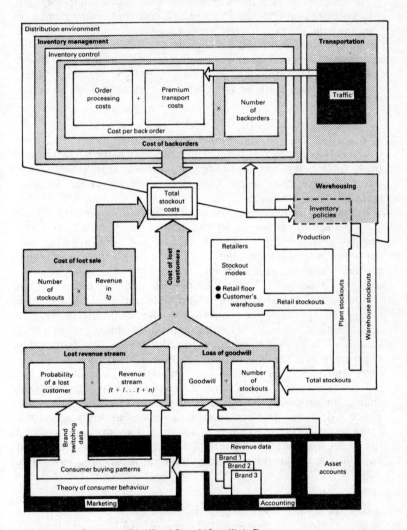

Source: Unpublished Master's Paper of J. Duane Weeks, *The Effect of Inventory Control and Stock-out Costs on the Management of a Multi-Echelon Distribution System* (University Park: Pennsylvania State University, 1974)

Figure 4.5   The cost of a stock-out

the total investment can be.

This inventory as well as representing a major component of total corporate assets (see Chapter 2) is a charge on the company from the time the raw materials etc. are paid for until the customer settles his invoice for the finished goods. While they are in the warehouse, in transit or work-in-progress they incur a cost. It has been suggested[1] that the cost of inventory comprises four elements: capital costs; service costs; storage costs, and risk costs.

Capital costs

The capital costs of inventory have two components, financing charges and opportunity costs. The financing charge should reflect the current cost of capital to the company and as such will clearly differ between companies. The opportunity cost arises because investment in inventory does not of itself produce a return, although it is sometimes argued that in times of rising prices there is such a return. However, in a successful business that inventory will have to be replaced at a higher cost thus negating any supposed benefit. If the capital tied up in inventory was available for use elsewhere, either within the company or outside, a return could be made on that capital. Depending upon the cost of capital to the company and any opportunity cost this could represent a charge of 20 per cent per annum of the value of the inventory. The question then arises: What is the appropriate basis for inventory valuation? Whatever the method used for producing a book value of inventory for the annual accounts of the company it is unlikely to be appropriate for logistics decision making. This is because the only costs relevant in this context are the incremental costs of a change in inventory levels. If a service level decision involves either a decrease or an increase in inventory at any stage in the chain, what costs have changed? Essentially we are talking about the direct costs of manufacturing or purchasing that inventory and any additional transport and handling costs incurred in moving it.

Service costs

Inventory service costs largely comprise stock management and insurance. In some countries, notably the USA, there is also a tax on inventory holding by corporations. In the UK current tax legislation can paradoxically make it advantageous to hold stock, at least at the year end! Stock management costs are often difficult to isolate particularly where computer-based systems are also used for, say, order processing and invoicing. Recent experience suggests that whilst the use of the computer in stock management has produced many improvements in efficiency it increases the actual costs of stock management. Certainly inventory service costs are by no means negligible.

Storage costs

Storage costs may often be accounted for separately, but since the only reason they will be incurred is to maintain inventory then logically they are an inventory-related cost. However, if the storage facilities are owned by the company and represent a fixed cost which is not influenced by the throughput of inventory, then that cost should be treated as sunk as we are concerned only with those that change as a result of changes in the level of inventory. On the other hand if public warehouses are used then normally a component of the charge will be volume related and thus affected by inventory level decisions. In the categorisation of logistics costs used in Chapter 1 all warehousing costs, other than those which vary with the volume of inventory stored, should be treated as 'facilities' rather than inventory costs.

Risk costs

Risk costs are generated through obsolescence, deterioration, damage and pilferage. Whilst they will vary from product to product and from time to time every attempt should be made to estimate them. Stock write-offs and losses incurred for whatever reason represent an important cost and one that is increasing.

These four cost categories taken together represent between 20 and 40 per cent of the incremental value of inventory at cost levels prevailing today. Even a relatively small business could acquire an annual bill of substantial magnitude given that inventory levels are typically high in relation to sales.[2]

Beyond the costs of inventory, however, the system must be capable of identifying all the costs of providing service to the customer. It can be argued therefore that more sophisticated approaches to identifying the costs of customer service are clearly required if improved logistics performance is to be achieved.

Principles of logistics costing

It will be apparent from the previous comments that the problem of developing an appropriate logistics-oriented costing system is primarily one of focus. That is the ability to focus upon the output of the distribution system, in essence the provision of customer service, and to identify the unique costs associated with that output. Traditional accounting methods lack this focus, mainly because they were designed with something else in mind.

One of the basic principles of logistics costing, it has been argued, is that the system should mirror the materials flow, i.e. it should be capable of identifying the costs that result from providing customer service in the marketplace. A second principle is that it should be capable of enabling separate cost and revenue analyses to be made by customer type and by market segment or distribution channel. This latter requirement emerges because of the dangers inherent in dealing solely with averages, e.g. the average cost per delivery, since they can conceal substantial variations either side of the mean.

To operationalise the first principle requires an 'output' orientation to costing. In other words first define the desired outputs of the distribution system and then seek to identify the costs associated with providing those outputs. A useful concept here is the idea of the 'mission'.[3] In the context of distribution, a mission is a set of goals to be achieved by the system within a specific product/market context. Missions can be defined in terms of the type of market served, by which products and within what

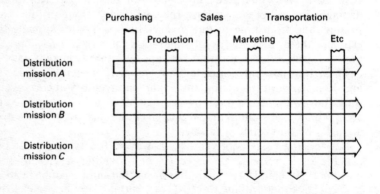

Mission A: To serve the company's Western European markets with a 95 per cent delivery within 10 days at lowest total costs.

Mission B: To serve the institutional buyers of the company's products, and to meet their stated requirements in terms of shipment sizes and delivery frequencies at lowest total cost.

Mission C: Meeting home consumer demand by utilising existing channels of distribution and operating facilities to maximise the logistics contribution to company profitability by a balancing of retailer service requirements against the cost involved.

Figure 4.6   Distribution missions that cut across functional boundaries

constraints of service and cost. A mission by its very nature cuts across traditional company lines. Figure 4.6 illustrates the concept and demonstrates the difference between an 'output' orientation based on missions and the 'input' orientation based on functions.

The successful achievement of defined mission goals involves inputs from a large number of functional areas and activity centres within the firm. Thus an effective distribution costing system must seek to determine the total systems cost of meeting desired distribution objectives (the 'outputs' of the system) and the costs of various inputs involved in meeting those outputs. Interest has been generated recently in an approach to this problem known as 'mission costing'.[4]

Figure 4.7 illustrates how three distribution missions may make a differential impact on activity centre/functional area costs and, in so doing, provide a logical basis for costing within the company. As a cost or budgeting method mission costing is the reverse of traditional techniques: under this scheme a functional budget is determined now by the demands of the missions it serves. Thus in figure 4.7 the cost per mission is identified horizontally and from this the functional budgets may be determined by summing vertically.

Given that the logic of mission costing is sound, how might it be made to work in practice? The pioneering work of Barrett[4] developed a framework for the application of mission costing. This approach requires firstly that all the activity centres associated with a particular distribution mission be identified, e.g. transport, warehousing, inventory etc., and secondly that the incremental costs for each activity centre incurred as a result of undertaking that mission must be isolated. Incremental costs are used because it is important not to take into account 'sunk' costs or those which would still be incurred even if the mission were abandoned. Barrett makes use of the idea of 'attributable costs':[5]

> Attributable cost is a cost per unit that could be avoided on average if a product or function were discontinued entirely without changing the supporting organisational structure.

In determining the costs of an activity centre, e.g. transport, attributable to a specific mission the question could be asked: What costs would we avoid if this customer/segment/channel were no longer serviced? These avoidable costs are the true incremental costs of servicing that customer/segment/channel. Often they will be substantially lower than the average cost because so many distribution costs are fixed and/or shared. For example, a vehicle leaves a depot in Luton to make deliveries in Nottingham and

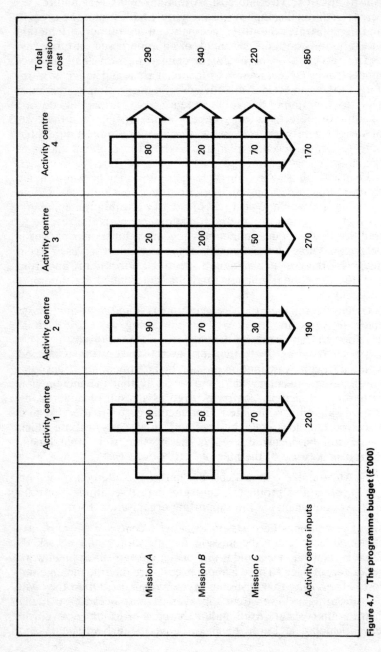

	Activity centre 1	Activity centre 2	Activity centre 3	Activity centre 4	Total mission cost
Mission A	100	90	20	80	290
Mission B	50	70	200	20	340
Mission C	70	30	50	70	220
Activity centre inputs	220	190	270	170	850

Figure 4.7   The programme budget (£'000)

Leeds. If those customers in Nottingham were abandoned, but those in Leeds retained, what would be the difference in the total cost of transport? The answer would be not very much. However, if the customers in Leeds were dropped, but not those in Nottingham, there would be a greater saving of costs because of the reduction in miles travelled.

With more complex delivery routes the same principles could be applied. To identify the costs of servicing individual customers a delivery routeing programme could be run, firstly to identify the least cost solution for servicing all customers (see figure 4.8(i)) within required service constraints. Next the routeing programme could be run again without customer 1 (C_1). This might produce quite a different route with a different total cost (see figure 4.8(ii)). The difference between the new cost and the previous cost could be seen as the transport costs attributable to that customer. A similar principle can be applied to identify the attributable costs of inventory, warehousing etc.

It might be argued that the flaw in this method is that if individual customer costs are identified by this method and added up the likelihood is that they will come to less than the known total cost. However, this difference could logically be defined as the common cost of servicing all customers and therefore is not relevant to the analysis.

This approach becomes particularly powerful when combined with a customer revenue analysis, because even customers with low sales offtake may still be profitable in incremental cost terms if not on an average cost basis. In other words the company would be worse off if those customers were abandoned.

Such insights as this can be gained by extending the mission costing concept to produce profitability analyses for customers, market segments or distribution channels. The term 'customer profitability accounting' describes any attempt to relate the revenue produced by a customer, market segment or distribution channel to the costs of servicing that customer/segment/channel.

Customer profitability accounting

It has long been recognised that the so-called 80/20 rule or 'Pareto's Law' holds when it comes to the profitability of customers. In other words most companies might expect something like 80 per cent of their total profit to come from only 20 per cent of their customers. Closer analysis of this data also reveals another 80/20 distribution. This time that 80 per cent of the total

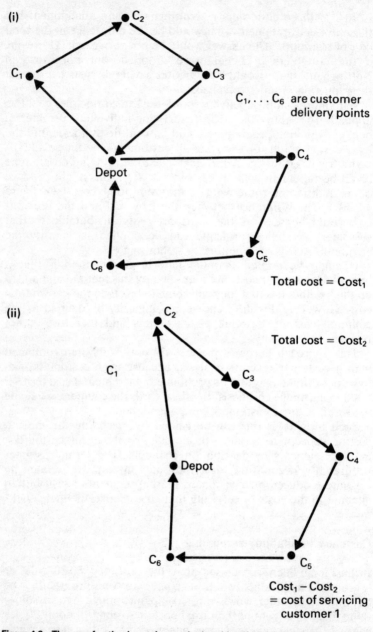

(i)

$C_1, \ldots C_6$ are customer delivery points

Total cost = $Cost_1$

(ii)

Total cost = $Cost_2$

$Cost_1 - Cost_2$
= cost of servicing customer 1

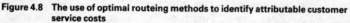

Figure 4.8   The use of optimal routeing methods to identify attributable customer service costs

costs of providing customer service are accounted for by only 20
per cent of the customers and also, more importantly, those 20 per
cent are not the same customers that appear in the top 20 per cent
by profitability.

This disparity in the costs of servicing different types of
customer can often be substantial. One study[6] gave an example of
customer servicing costs as a percentage of net sales for one
company's customers:

	Low	Average	High
Order processing	0.2	2.6	7.4
Inventory carrying	1.1	2.6	10.2
Picking and shipping	0.3	0.7	2.5
Interplant freight and handling	0.0	1.5	7.6
Outbound freight	2.8	7.1	14.1
Discounts	2.4	3.1	4.4

Data such as this provides further justification for not using
averages when it comes to calculating distribution costs. On the
other hand it is a fairly daunting task to attempt to identify the
costs of individual accounts, other than large or 'key' accounts.
However, it should be feasible to group customers by size, type,
market segment or mission and take a representative sample to at
least gain some insight into the real costs of servicing different
types of customer.

What sort of costs should be taken into account in this type of
analysis? Figure 4.9 presents a basic model which attempts to
identify only those customer-related costs which are avoidable
(i.e. if the customer did not exist, those costs would not be
incurred).

The starting point is the gross sales value of the order from
which is then subtracted the discounts that are given on that order
to the customer. This leaves the net sales value from which must
be taken the direct production costs or cost of goods sold. Indirect
costs are not allocated unless they are fully attributable to that
customer. The same principle applies to sales and marketing costs
as attempts to allocate indirect costs, such as national advertising,
can only be done on an arbitrary and usually misleading basis. The
attributable distribution costs can then be assigned to give
customer gross contribution. Finally any other customer-related
costs, such as trade credit, returns etc. are subtracted to give a net
contribution to overheads and profit. Often the figure that
emerges as the 'bottom line' can be revealing as shown in table 4.1.

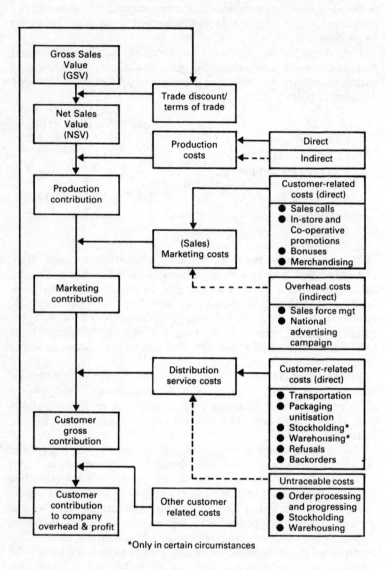

*Only in certain circumstances

Figure 4.9 Customer profitability accounting

Table 4.1
Analysis of revenue and cost for a specific customer

	£	£
Gross sales value		100,000
Less discount	10,000	
Net sales value		90,000
Less direct cost of goods sold	20,000	
Gross contribution		70,000
Less sales and marketing costs:		
Sales calls	3,000	
Co-operative promotions	1,000	
Merchandising	3,000	
	7,000	
		63,000
Less distribution costs:		
Order processing	500	
Storage and handling	600	
Inventory financing	700	
Transport	2,000	
Packaging	300	
Refusals	500	
	4,600	
Customer gross contribution		58,400
Less other customer-related costs:		
Credit financing	1,500	
Returns	500	
	2,000	
Customer net contribution		56,400

In this case a gross contribution of £70,000 becomes a net contribution of £56,400 as soon as the costs unique to this customer are taken into account. If the analysis were to be extended by attempting to allocate overheads (a step not to be advised because of the problems usually associated with such allocation) what might at first sight seem to be a profitable customer could be deemed to be the reverse. However, as long as the net contribution is positive and there is no 'opportunity cost' in servicing that customer the company would be better off with the business than without it.

The value of this type of exercise can be substantial. The information could be used firstly when the next sales contract is negotiated and, secondly, as the basis for sales and marketing strategy in directing effort away from less profitable types of account towards more profitable business. More importantly it can point the way to alternative strategies for managing customers with high servicing costs to improve their profitability as the following example demonstrates.

* * * * * * *

Case study: The distributor option[6]

A speciality chemicals company which was operating at an overall loss found that only the top 7 per cent of its customers brought in profitable business, and that sales and distribution costs were the key to the losses. Greater volume per customer would alleviate much of the problem, but this was not really an attainable solution as the company was already the prime supplier to most of its customers. That left two choices: the company could either drop the majority of its customers, or it could find some way to reduce sales and distribution costs. The first option was discarded because of its undesirable effect on the costs of production. The best way to realise the second option appeared to be by switching some customers to outside distribution contractors.

The distributor option was analysed using the base data on customer profitability, and taking account of the cost of serving the new distributors, including their margin. It appeared that break-even could be achieved if 60 per cent of the customers were transferred to distributors. Clearly, however, the best decision would be the one generating maximum profit. This was the point at which 90 per cent of the customers were serviced by distributors, and only 10 per cent directly by the company. Interestingly, the solution meant keeping as direct customers some accounts that were only contributing to overheads and not actually generating profits for the company.

A thorough analysis indicated that several factors, including product mix, delivery frequency and discounts, had much the same degree of impact on the losses that were being incurred. It also emerged that the terms of trade of the non-contributing customers were negotiated centrally between the company and its customers' head offices: the issues in the negotiations being, of course, volume and discount. Because certain customers took very large volumes, they were able to secure very substantial discounts. However, when the company looked at deliveries to individual outlets, which were retail stores, a different picture emerged. Volumes were modest, frequency was high and products were mainly lower priced, low margin items.

Once this was understood, the company was able to approach the next round of negotiations in an informed fashion, to agree terms of trade and to take account of the real variables that influenced its profitability. Instead of negotiating only on the basis of the total order, consideration was given to the customers' requirements for delivery to each outlet. Customers accepted that delivery to numerous outlets was a costly exercise, and should be a factor in the negotiations.

* * * * * *

Other ways of improving customer profitability once this basic information is to hand are by encouraging the customer to order in larger quantities; by attempting to improve the consolidation of deliveries either by reducing the delivery frequency or by improving the planning of deliveries through better use of order cycle time; attempting to improve the product mix so that the customer takes more higher margin products; and by cutting back on selling costs. Whatever the appropriate strategy the need for it is unlikely to be recognised unless some system of customer accounting is installed.

Notes

1   D. M. Lambert, *The Development of an Inventory Costing Methodology: A Study of the Costs Associated with Holding Inventory*, National Council of Physical Distribution Management, Chicago, Illinois, 1976.
2   D. Ray and S. Millman, 'Optimal Inventories via Customer Service Objectives' in *International Journal of Physical Distribution and Materials Management*, vol. 9, no. 7, 1979.
3   M. Christopher, *Total Distribution: A Framework for Analysis, Costing and Control*, Gower, 1971.
4   T. Barrett, 'Mission Costing: A New Approach to Logistics Analysis' in *International Journal of Physical Distribution and Materials Management*, vol. 12, no. 7, 1982.
5   G. Shillinglaw, 'The Concept of Attributable Cost' in *Journal of Accounting Research*, vol. 1, no. 1, Spring 1963.
6   G. V. Hill and D. A. Harland, 'The Customer Profit Centre' in *Focus*, The Journal of the Institute of Physical Distribution Management, vol. 2, no. 2, May/June 1983.

5 Auditing distribution performance

Understanding the present position is a prerequisite for improving the future, which is certainly the case in logistics management. The very complexity and diversity of logistics within the firm often disguises the real situation. For example, the real costs of processing an order may not be known because they are spread across several functions. It may be that some of the component costs, such as order entry and order picking are known, but others, e.g. credit checking and invoicing are not. Again these costs may be known in aggregate but not by customer type or market channel.

To overcome these knowledge gaps and to improve the basis for logistics decision making it is necessary to establish a procedure for the generation of relevant and timely information relating to the current status of the logistics system. This is the notion of the 'distribution audit'. It is not an audit in the accounting sense which serves the purpose of verifying the company's accounts, rather it is a regular and systematic review of distribution performance in terms of costs, resource utilisation and service outputs. It should be conducted regularly to provide indications of trends and should be systematic to ensure that maximum information is derived from the available data.

The audit task can be seen as one of converting data into information and to achieve this the appropriate data base must exist and likewise the procedures for extracting the desired information. Chapter 6 will concentrate upon the procedures for developing the logistics information system, but first the nature of the distribution audit needs to be clearly understood.

The need to audit

Two reasons for establishing a distribution auditing procedure are firstly to improve control and secondly to improve productivity in the logistics function.

Even the best organised systems will require control to ensure that the desired outputs are achieved and that the use of inputs (resources) is within the planned levels. Variations from planned levels will occur with both the inputs and the outputs due to a variety of reasons. It is convenient to categorise these variations into 'internal' and 'external' environments. The internal environment relates to those variables within the control of the firm, e.g. product mix, system configuration, procedures etc. The external environment concerns those elements generally beyond the control of the company, e.g. customer requirements, competitors' service policy, government legislation etc. Thus to improve the control of the logistics system both the external and internal environments must be monitored, along with the measurement of resource inputs and performance outputs.

The second reason for establishing a distribution auditing procedure is to assist in the search for productivity improvements in the logistics function. Productivity may simply be defined as the ratio of the outputs of a system to the inputs. In the logistics context we can think of customer service performance as the output and the logistics mix elements (e.g. inventory, storage and handling, transportation, order processing etc.) as the inputs. Improvements in productivity require first an understanding of the present position and secondly an identification of the possibilities for improvement. Again the need for an audit becomes imperative.

Studies carried out for the National Council of Physical Distribution Management[1] in the USA and the Centre for Physical Distribution Management[2] in the UK have identified the great opportunities for improvements in logistics productivity. The US study reported that as much as $40 billion a year could be saved in total distribution costs. This level of cost reduction was thought to be achievable on average across all US firms. The UK study identified a similar opportunity for a 10 per cent improvement in costs leading in this case to an overall saving of £2,000 million.

The dual role of the distribution audit is illustrated in figure 5.1, which suggests that the role of the audit is to monitor outputs and inputs against predetermined performance standards and identify corrective action where necessary.

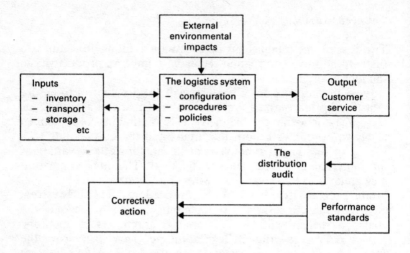

Figure 5.1   The distribution audit as a means of monitoring and controlling logistics performance and productivity

The NCPDM study[1] referred to above defined productivity in distribution as being measured by the 'ratio of real output produced to real resources consumed'. For example, typical measures might be:

Cases picked per man hour.
Orders delivered per vehicle day.
Orders processed per shift.

Table 5.1 identifies some of the key input and output elements encountered in distribution.

As the NCPDM study pointed out not all of the measures commonly used in industry to track productivity are input/output measures. They defined two other measures as 'utilisation' and 'performance' and provided the following definitions:

Productivity is the ratio of real output to real input, e.g. cases per labour hour.
Utilisation is the ratio of capacity used to available capacity, e.g. percentage of pallet spaces occupied in a warehouse.
Performance is the ratio of actual output to standard output, e.g. cases picked per hour versus standard hourly pick rate.

The same report suggested that the measures used in a distribution audit must meet as many as possible of the following criteria to be

Table 5.1
Inputs and outputs of the logistics system

Inputs	Outputs
Human resources	*Service levels*
Hourly labour	Lead times
Salaried staff	Reliability
Management	Order fill rates
	Sales units
	Orders
Physical resources	Shipment
Land, buildings	Deliveries
Depots	Invoices
Equipment	Line items
	Units
	Pieces
Financial resources	Dozens
Inventories	Cases
Accounts receivable	Cartons
	Pallet loads
	Truck loads
Energy	*Weight/volume*
Fuel	Kilogrammes
Power	Tonnes
	Cubic metres
	Density
	Value
	Cost of goods sold
	Sales value
	Value added

of value in improving productivity:

Validity The measurement must accurately reflect changes in productivity.

Coverage The more completely a measure or measures encompass all uses of a resource, the more fully it can be tracked and its productivity measured.

Comparability To be trackable, a productivity measure must be reduced to a common denominator, typically to standard units of output/input or to standard hours of work.

Completeness The thoroughness with which all important

resources are measured consistent with the specific application.

Usefulness   A measure must focus management attention on the productivity issues. The measure must help guide the manager toward effective action.

Compatibility   The more compatible a measure is to existing data and information flows in an organisation, the easier it will be to implement.

Cost effectiveness   It makes no sense to spend more collecting measurement data than can be gained through its use.

When is an audit necessary?

Ideally the distribution audit should be seen as a continuing activity which provides insight into logistics performance. Realistically however major reviews of the total distribution system will be time-consuming and costly. A distinction therefore needs to be made between the performance feedback data necessary for day-to-day management control of the logistics system and the more strategic reviews of the distribution system which will, by their nature, be required less often. The type of situations that might prompt the latter, strategic distribution audit could be for example:

> When the company makes a significant change in its marketing strategy (for example, selling direct to end users rather than through intermediaries).

> When the size of the business changes significantly either organically or through acquisition or divestiture.

> When new product lines or major customers are added or when old products are discontinued or major customers lost.

> When the company's geographic mix of shipments changes appreciably.

> When five years have passed since the last strategic evaluation

Further indications that the distribution system may be in need of review can be signalled by conditions such as:

> *Inventories that turn slowly*   Finished goods inventory should turn between six and twelve times a year in most situations. Stock turns of less than six times a year are a frequent sign of

control problems.

Poor customer service As a rule of thumb maintaining finished goods inventory at a level equivalent to two months' sales should provide a service level of about 99 per cent. One month's inventory cover should provide about 90 per cent service. Failure to achieve these service levels could mean that the inventory is in the wrong products, the wrong location, or both.

Inter-warehouse shipments Because stock transfers require double handling and incur additional transport costs, movements between warehouses should be carefully monitored and any significant changes in the level and pattern should signal attention.

Premium freight charges Again if the level of transport costs incurred by the use of 'emergency' type freight rise, this will indicate basic problems in the distribution system which need investigation.

The distinction made earlier between the 'strategic' distribution audit and the more performance or 'tactically' oriented review is a convenient one for the purposes of explanation, even if in reality the distinction between them is somewhat blurred. The following sections expand upon the nature of these two complementary aspects of the distribution audit.

The strategic distribution audit

There is a close link between marketing and distribution strategy even though this may not always be recognised within the organisation. There is a need to integrate distribution planning more closely with marketing planning, as will be shown in Chapter 9. Decisions taken regarding distribution networks and channels can have a signficant impact on marketplace performance. The role of the strategic distribution audit therefore should be to examine the appropriateness of the existing distribution strategy for the achievement of the company's marketing objectives.

In recent years there has been an increasing concern amongst corporate and marketing planners with competitive analysis (see, for example, the work of Michael Porter[3]). This is a recognition that in markets exhibiting little growth, or even decline, the only way forward for a company is to win market share from the competition, which in turn means factoring the competitive environment into the individual company's strategy. The forces

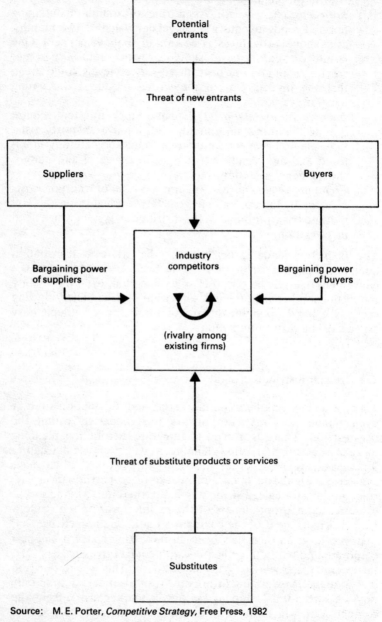

Source: M. E. Porter, *Competitive Strategy*, Free Press, 1982

Figure 5.2   Forces driving industry competition

driving industry competition are shown using Porter's framework in figure 5.2.

This framework can be easily adapted as the basis for the strategic distribution audit. Firstly there is the need to review thoroughly the existing competitive profile, e.g. the number and location of competitors, their strengths and weaknesses, their service offering and their distribution strategy. Such information is often easy to come by. Surprisingly few companies keep detailed files on their competitors, nor try to develop 'scenarios' of likely competitive actions. Compare this with, say, the manager of a First Division football club preparing his team for a cup final. He will have available to him video tapes of all the previous games played that season by the competing side. A detailed 'form book' will have been maintained on each member of the competing squad. Every favourite tactic of the competition will be analysed in detail. The analogy with competitive analysis in business is remarkably strong.

Following this detailed appraisal of competitive strategy the other forces impinging upon the company's strategy must be examined. It is conventional to consider these forces under the heading of the 'external environment'. In the development of distribution strategy close attention must be paid to the environment and to those many external forces within it that can change so rapidly and negate even the most carefully planned system.

Figure 5.3 lists the four key areas where external changes could have the greatest impact upon a company's distribution performance. They cover the market, the competition, the marketing channel and the legal framework. Other areas could have been added to this list, particularly distribution technology (which for convenience here has been included in the channel profile). The fact that changes on any of these dimensions can radically affect the cost and performance of a logistics system means that they must be very carefully monitored. So often changes in these areas will be gradual and may pass unnoticed, yet the ultimate effect upon the system could be profound. For example there have been many changes in distribution channels. Twenty years ago most toothpaste was bought at chemists, now almost all toothpaste is bought at supermarkets. Ten years ago the supermarkets' share of the alcoholic beverage market was negligible, now they are the biggest retailers of wine in the UK. Even in industrial markets there have been a surprising number of changes in the routes that products take to markets. Who would have thought ten years ago that there would ever be a volume retail business for computer sales? Changes such as these have

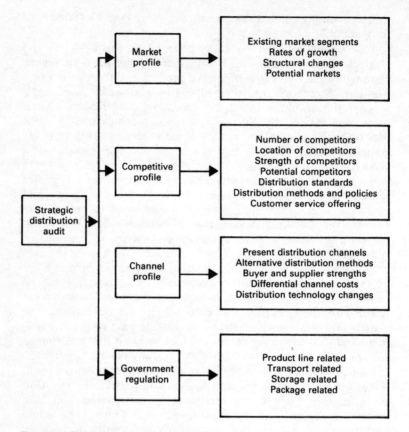

Figure 5.3 External environment appraisal

major implications for a manufacturer and the determination of appropriate distribution strategies.

Another example which had major implications for distribution was the change in the UK legal environment following the adoption of the EEC Common Transport policy, particularly as it relates to the eight-hour driving day. Many companies had to rethink their entire transportation strategy to enable service levels to be maintained without unacceptable cost increases.

It is rarely the case that changes such as these in the external environment happen suddenly, without warning. Usually the trends are visible or advance knowledge can be gained, but only if a formal and systematic attempt is made to monitor such trends. Thus the need for the strategic distribution audit.

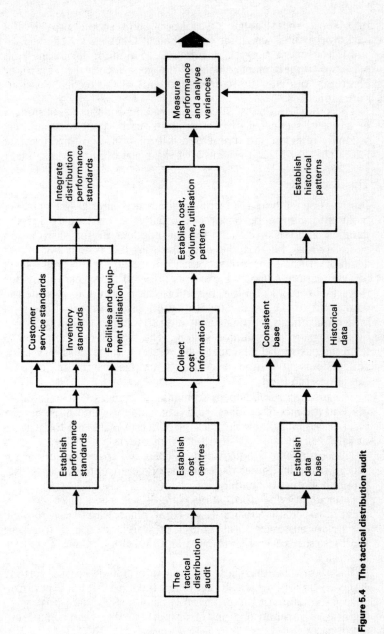

Figure 5.4 The tactical distribution audit

The tactical distribution audit

Establish performance standards
- Customer service standards
- Inventory standards
- Facilities and equipment utilisation

Integrate distribution performance standards

Establish cost centres

Collect cost information

Establish cost, volume, utilisation patterns

Establish data base
- Consistent base
- Historical data

Establish historical patterns

Measure performance and analyse variances

87

The tactical distribution audit

In a sense the strategic distribution audit should provide the backdrop against which the tactical audit takes place. The tactical audit, as its name suggests, is primarily to monitor deviations from plan and to alert management of the need for corrective action. Figure 5.4 outlines the basic components of the tactical distribution audit.

There are essentially three requirements for the establishment of a useful tactical distribution audit: firstly a set of standards; secondly relevant and timely cost information, and thirdly a data base. This latter requirement is at the heart of any audit model.

The data base

Information gathered for conventional accounting and management information purposes will usually be inadequate for the detailed analysis necessary for the conduct of the distribution audit. It may be that the data exists in the system but is not available in the appropriate form, or it may be at too high a level of aggregation. Chapter 6 explores in detail the requirements for the establishment of a logistics information system to provide the vital input to the management of the logistics process. The data base requirement for the tactical audit should most sensibly be met by the logistics information system. The type of data required to form the basis for the tactical audit relates to materials flows, costs and systems utilisation. Figure 5.5 summarises the major data categories required.

The *product profile* needs to highlight changes that have taken place in the mix of products sold (e.g. value/weight ratios, density etc.), seasonality, new product introduction plans and the pattern of sales (e.g. frequency distribution of orders).

The *cost profile* will identify unit costs and cost distributions for order processing, outer packaging, storage, inventory, transportation and materials handling.

Data identifying *distribution patterns* will need to cover shipment flow characteristics (e.g. from plant warehouse to field depots to customers), utilisation of warehouses and transport facilities, service levels achieved and inventory balances at stock locations.

The data base must also include information on the existing *system capability* which should detail the capacities and performance parameters of the order processing system, data processing facilities, warehousing and transport facilities and materials handling facilities.

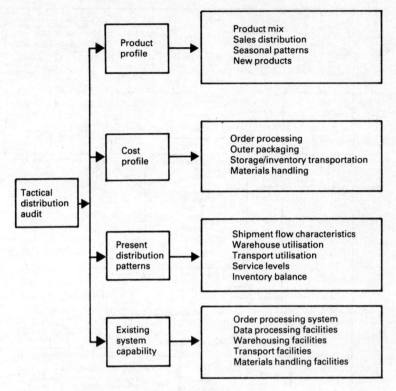

Figure 5.5   The tactical distribution audit data base

The distribution data base is nothing more than a store of facts about the distribution system which can be regularly updated and which can provide rapid access to basic operating statistics. Ideally a 'distribution system fact book' should be maintained which enables management to locate key, up-to-date information with a minimum of difficulty.

Establishing cost centres

The need to establish appropriate distribution cost accounting systems for more effective logistics management was emphasised in Chapter 4 and certainly it is a key requirement for the distribution audit.

Accurate and timely cost information is required on each of the logistics 'activity' centres, primarily: transport, storage, inventory, order processing and materials handling/utilisation and related

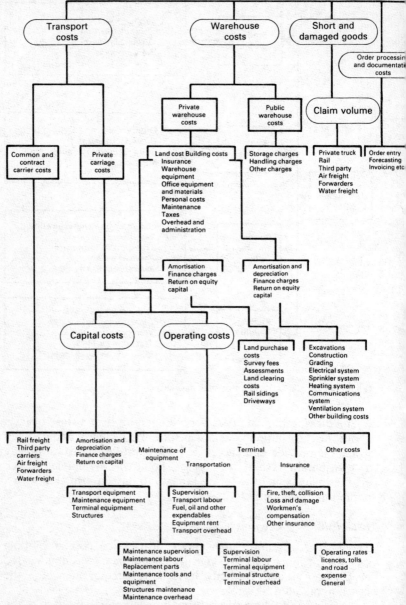

Source: Based upon William B. Saunders, 'Designing a Distribution System' in *Distribution Age,* January 1965, pp. 32-36.

Figure 5.6 Distribution cost centres

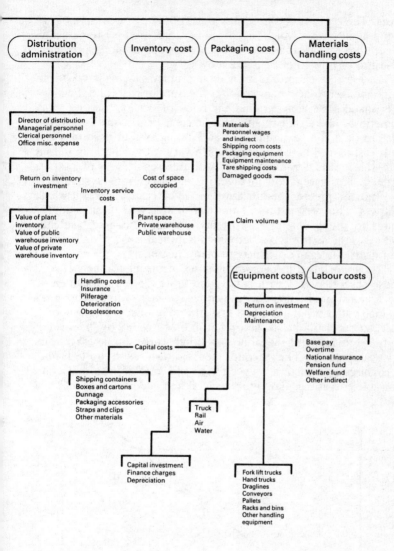

costs. These are broad headings and within lie a great number of component costs which need to be measured systematically. Figure 5.6 reveals the cost elements which combine to provide a measure of how total costs are moving.

The previous chapter identified the problems facing the distribution manager in achieving a better measure of costs and the point was made that conventional methods of cost accounting may sometimes make that relationship unclear or provide a distorted picture of it. For example, the accounting system used may not fully distinguish between costs which vary with changes in output and those which remain fixed over different levels of output. Indeed the aggregation involved in the accounting system may prevent the precise identification of which costs vary with which outputs. The very nature of the distribution activity also contributes to the problems of cost accounting. The heterogeneous nature of the distribution 'output' adds difficulties, e.g. one vehicle can distribute many products to many customers.

The importance in decision making of distinguishing between those costs that vary with output and those that do not can easily be demonstrated. Figure 5.7 illustrates two views of how costs may change with output. The first one, the solid line, is based upon a calculation of total costs at a point in time divided by the level of output prevailing at that time – in other words, an 'average total cost' approach. The second view, shown as a dotted line, recognises a distinction between fixed and variable costs and a unit variable cost is calculated to which is then added a constant fixed cost.

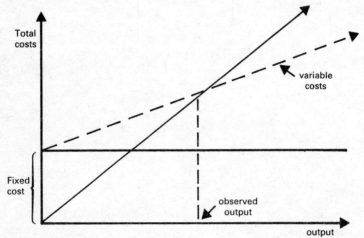

Figure 5.7   Fixed and variable costs

The difference between fixed and variable costs is underlined when decisions are made regarding changes in the level of output (which could be taken in the distribution context to be the level of service). For expansions in output (improvements in the level of service) the relevant concept is the incremental cost of expanding that service, which may or may not involve additional fixed costs. In reducing output (reduction in service level) the relevant concept is 'avoidable' cost, in other words those which will no longer be incurred. Both these decisions can only be made sensibly if there is some knowledge of the difference between fixed and variable costs.

To overcome these problems of separating fixed and variable cost elements in distribution activities an approach known as 'statistical costing'[4] may be used. This relies upon the use of statistical techniques, usually multiple regression analysis, to derive cost estimating relationships from a sample of actual operating experiences. For example, the cost of running a warehouse would be related to the various inputs involved such as cube utilisation, throughput, labour, materials handling etc. Data relating to the measured level of total warehousing costs would be related through regression analysis to these input categories in such a way that any variation in total costs could be analysed in terms of changes in input levels.

A simplistic example is where total distribution costs are related to just one variable, throughput, measured in tons/month. Data is collected on total distribution costs, however they may be defined, over, say, a 24-month period and for each of those months throughput is also recorded. If these data were plotted in the form of a scatter diagram something like the relationship in figure 5.8 might emerge.

Regression analysis enables the analyst to fit a line or a curve to this data in such a way that it provides a statistical description of any implied relationship that may underlie it. This line of 'best fit' is superimposed on the scatter in figure 5.7. It is of the form:

$$y = a + bx$$

Where y equals total distribution costs, the x is throughput/month. This can be interpreted as follows: a represents the fixed costs element in the system, i.e. the point at which the line intersects the y axis, and b represents the variable cost associated with each unit of throughput, i.e. the slope of the line.

It will be apparent that such a simplistic level of analysis as suggested in this example is fraught with danger. Such a high level of aggregation is implied in both variables used here, i.e. 'total

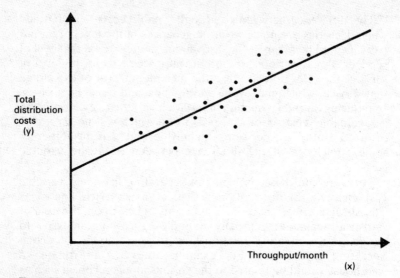

Figure 5.8   Regression analysis of distribution costs

distribution costs' and 'throughput/month', that the analysis tells us nothing about how total costs vary with the specific activities involved in generating 'throughput/month'. Similarly in order to obtain a value for *a* (fixed costs) we have extrapolated backwards outside the range of our observations, which may or may not be a valid assumption. However, these are not criticisms against the method itself, merely examples of some of the possible pitfalls in its use.

The analysis would normally include a number of variables. For example, in a survey of warehousing costs in a particular industry in Holland, data was gathered as follows:

C = total warehousing cost in guilders (00,000s)
N = number of warehouses
A = area covered by system in sq. km. (0,000s)
T = tonnage through system (0,000s)

Company	C	N	A	T
1	4.40	1	1.1	6.4
2	14.11	6	6.2	24.7
3	5.37	2	2.8	17.5
4	13.45	4	7.9	26.1
5	4.60	1	0.9	14.2
6	9.79	3	4.6	25.4

Company	C	N	A	T
7	9.88	3	6.1	16.9
8	5.44	2	1.6	7.3
9	3.47	1	2.2	5.8
10	15.44	5	9.6	18.6
11	5.52	1	1.7	14.0
12	9.55	4	3.4	22.2
13	17.65	6	10.5	28.9
14	6.00	2	1.0	6.2
15	6.75	2	2.8	8.8

Using multiple regression analysis the following relationship was derived:

$$C = 1.45 + 1.3N + 0.06A^2 + 0.5 \sqrt{T}$$

This implies a fixed cost of 145,000 guilders with a linear relationship between total costs and the number of warehouses, but with non-linear relationships between total costs and area served and likewise for system throughput.

Analysis such as this makes possible a much clearer interpretation of the raw data. It pinpoints the relative influence on total costs of variation in each of the input variables and, within the constraints of the model, it enables the impact of different combinations of inputs on total costs to be assessed.

This example was based upon a 'cross-section' analysis of data whereby similar entities, in this case warehouse systems within the same industry, are compared at a single point in time. Other examples could be a comparison of operating costs for individual warehouses within a single firm's system, or an analysis of costs of serving different types of customer. The cross-section approach contrasts with the 'time-series' approach which was used in the early example in which data for the same system was gathered over a period of time.

Establishing performance standards

By themselves cost and volume data are not sufficient for the establishment of a tactical distribution audit. There have to be benchmarks against which performance can be measured. These may be described as standards and they produce the indicators of what performance levels the system is expected to achieve.

The derivation of standards in distribution is difficult. Against what should performance be measured? Achievements in the past, competitive performance, arbitrary targets, or what?

A number of methods exist which may be used, individually or in combination, to produce performance standards. As far as cost standards are concerned it can often be helpful to use the statistical costing methods described previously to provide an empirical measure of costs. However there are shortcomings to this method – particularly problematic is the fact that regression-derived relationships may only hold over the range of values measured. For example, if volumes were to move above or below this range of previous measurement then the same relationships may not apply.

The use of industrial engineering methods to identify 'theoretical' achievable standards may be of some help particularly when setting volume and throughput standards.[5] Comparative data, either from other parts of the same company or from competing companies, can also help establish guidelines for setting distribution standards. Various organisations offer comparative data of this sort, for example the Centre for Interfirm Comparison and the Centre for Physical Distribution Management in the UK and Herbert Davis & Co. in the USA. Whilst there may be substantial differences in structure between companies in the same industry which can make comparisons difficult, information of this sort can provide a starting point for the setting of standards.

There are a number of general principles which should be observed when establishing performance standards. Perhaps the most important is that allowance should be made for the measurement system to take into account changes in volume against budgeted levels. For example if distribution costs in total are over budget in a period by 10 per cent, but the volume shipped is greater than anticipated by 12 per cent, is this good or bad? Unless we have a monitoring system that breaks down costs into fixed and variable components and then relates the variable costs to volume that question cannot be answered. To help with this type of problem many distribution managers have installed flexible budgeting systems which identify the fixed and variable components of costs in order to identify those which will be influenced by volume variances. A revised standard cost is then calculated based upon the actual volume that was achieved. A simplified example of a flexible distribution budget is shown in table 5.2. What at first sight appeared to be a substantial negative variance on budget becomes a small positive variance when volume changes are factored into the budget. This illustrates the importance of setting up a distribution auditing system which monitors real rather than apparent changes in system performance.

It is not only standards for cost and volume that need to be established, but also for service levels and facilities utilisation. The service level question was considered in Chapter 3. The establishment of utilisation standards requires an analysis of maximum activity levels for each logistics facility, e.g. depots, vehicles, containers etc. This is necessary if inaccurate conclusions are to be avoided from the appraisal of operating data. For example, if the capacity of a vehicle fleet is 1,000 pallet loads a day and we receive and ship 1,000 pallets in a day a simple productivity measure of, say, pallets shipped : pallets ordered would give 100 per cent. If demand increased one day to 1,500 pallets but our capacity remained fixed, then the ratio would fall to 66 per cent – on the face of it a fall in productivity! Because the efficient utilisation of logistics facilities is central to cost-effective distribution it is essential that firstly maximum operating capacities are known and secondly that actual utilisation be carefully monitored.

Table 5.2
A flexible distribution budget

Variations from fixed budget at warehouse

	Actual £	Budget £	Variance £
Variable costs			
Overtime	1,500	–	(1,500)
Temporary labour	500	–	(500)
Telephone	400	350	(50)
Postage	300	270	(30)
Packaging and shipping			
materials	1,000	800	(200)
Transport (third party)	5,000	4,000	(1,000)
Fixed costs			
Wages	7,000	7,000	–
Rent	500	500	–
Insurance	100	100	–
Rates	50	50	–
	£16,350	£13,070	£(3,280)

Budget activity: 800 cases shipped
Actual activity: 1,000 cases shipped

(Table 5.2 continued)

Variations for flexible budget at warehouse

	Actual	Flexible budget for 1,000 cases	Variance
	£	£	£
Variable costs			
Overtime	1,500	1,500	–
Temporary labour	500	500	–
Telephone	400	438	38
Postage	300	338	38
Packaging and shipping material	1,000	1,000	–
Transport (third party)	5,000	5,000	–
Fixed costs			
Wages	7,000	7,000	–
Rent	500	500	–
Insurance	100	100	–
Rates	50	50	–
	£16,350	£16,426	£76

Budget activity: 800 cases shipped
Actual activity: 1,000 cases shipped

Summary

The three components of the tactical distribution audit – the data base, cost centre information and performance standards – must come together through a formal monitoring and review programme. The use of simple indicators should be sufficient to signal the need for further investigation and corrective actions. One of the standard works on the distribution audit[6] recommends a simple series of interlinked ratios, each one summarising key information on operating performance. With the advent of widespread availability of computer-based performance monitoring the need to keep things simple becomes ever more urgent as the amount of information available grows exponentially.

Notes

1 *Measuring Productivity in Physical Distribution*, National Council of Physical Distribution Management, Chicago, 1978.
2 *Improving Productivity in Physical Distribution*, Centre for Physical Distribution Management, London, 1980.
3 Michael E. Porter, *Competitive Strategy: Techniques for Analyzing Industries and Competitors*, Free Press, 1980.
4 J. Johnston, *Statistical Costing*, McGraw Hill, 1960.
5 H. M. Armitage and J. F. Dickow, 'Controlling Distribution with Standard Costs and Flexible Budgets', National Council of Physical Distribution Management, Annual Conference Proceedings, 1979.
6 M. Christopher, D. Walters and J. Gattorna, *Distribution Planning and Control*, Gower, 1977.

6 Logistics information systems

At the heart of an efficiently managed materials flow there has to be an efficiently managed flow of information. Information is the trigger function for the logistics system as well as being vital for its maintenance. Information is what keeps the materials flow system 'open' in the sense that it is capable of adjusting to new circumstances. Any system that does not incorporate a feedback and control element, i.e. it is 'closed', succumbs eventually to entropy or decay. To provide a responsive, customer-oriented logistics system it is therefore necessary to ensure that the physical system is paralleled by an information system. The information system needs to produce timely and relevant information which can provide the basis for logistical response and, where necessary, corrective management action.

A distinction needs to be drawn between information and data. So often the two are confused, and indeed the manager is often surrounded by data without having much information. Data are facts, discrete items which may lack the necessary integration or ordering that produces information. It is the organisation of data that liberates the information contained within them. The distinction is easily understood if we consider a telephone directory. Each name and address with a telephone number alongside it is an item of data. If those data items were simply printed in the directory in random order it would be extremely difficult to find a specific individual's telephone number. Once the names are placed in alphabetical order however we have a very efficient source of information. The same data is involved but by giving order to the data the information is liberated. To continue the analogy, unless the telephone company regularly updates the directory the information contained will gradually lose its timeliness and relevance and will ultimately 'decay' as a source of information.

relevance and will ultimately 'decay' as a source of information.

One further element for definition remains and that is the concept of an information system. A system might simply be defined as a device for converting an input into an output. An information system normally uses multiple inputs, i.e. data from many sources, and processes and integrates that data to give specified information outputs. For example, demand for a particular item might be recorded at each sales point in the logistics system, amalgamated, trends established and then compared with records of stock on hand and planned production levels to provide an output of projected stock availability. This can then provide the basis for management action.

The system is therefore the means whereby data can be stored and processed in order to convert it into information. We are used to thinking of systems as being synonymous with computers, but this need not necessarily be so. The simplest systems may be capable of manual operation and maintenance, but the complexity and volume of the data required to establish a logistics information system usually means that computerisation is essential. In any case the reduction in the real costs of computing has made it possible for even the smallest business to contemplate the installation of a computer-based information system.

Information needs

What information should the system provide? Given sufficient resources and availability of data there would be no limit to the information that could be generated. The design of a logistics information system must begin with an audit of information needs against stringent cost/benefit criteria. This means that the key decision taken by logistics personnel must be identified and the question asked: 'What information is required in order that this decision can be made, bearing in mind the cost of acquiring that information?' Ultimately the decision to acquire information has to be the result of a balance between the costs involved against the benefits of reduced risk as a result of having the appropriate information to hand. For example, the costs of setting up an improved demand forecasting capability have to be weighed against the costs of a stock-out. This balance is not easy to calculate as so many of the risks are difficult to quantify. Nevertheless care must be taken against over-investment in sophisticated information systems where the risk costs are low as well as the reverse situation.

The same cost/benefit issues arise when the question of information storage is confronted. There is always the danger of a rapid escalation of costs as a result of storing data in a system that may only have a marginal value for later retrieval. For example, how frequently should customer files be 'cleaned' of historical data?

There are similar problems concerning speed of system response. Some real-time information systems monitor moment-by-moment changes in the physical system, for example, an airline reservation system. However, it may be more appropriate to work in a batch processing mode which updates daily but which might lead to lags in the response system.

These and other questions can only be answered after a careful analysis of the real managerial requirements for information. It has to be recognised that there are different levels of information requirements which in a sense mirror the typical decision-making hierarchy of the firm. Figure 6.1 depicts the way in which the output of the logistics information system should ideally mirror the use to which that information is put at the different levels of the corporate hierarchy.

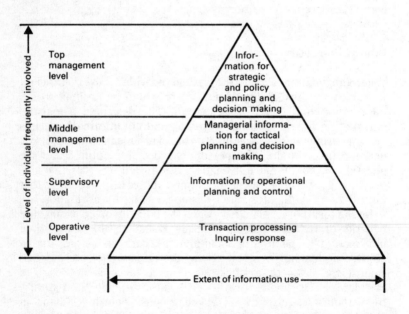

Figure 6.1 Hierarchy of use for the logistics information system (LIS)

If these various output requirements are to be met by a single, integrated logistics information system, then the data base around which it is constructed must reflect this diversity. A basic principle in information system design is that the data should be collected firstly at the lowest level of aggregation and secondly it must be dimensionally compatible. The reason for seeking disaggregated data is to enable subsequent aggregations to be made with the greatest degree of flexibility. It is always frustrating to find, for example, that data on sales is only available at a national level whereas a particular analysis requires regional trends to be computed. Secondly for different sets of data to be merged or compared there is a requirement for dimensional compatibility, thus if the decision maker wishes to compare brand shares with service levels then the time periods in which they are measured must equate.

The complete logistics information system will be a complex set of data which is capable of manipulation and analysis in as many ways as are required by the logistics manager. More often than not the system must incorporate the capability for more detailed statistical analysis to be performed. At the end of it all there must be an output which makes sense in terms of the decisions that have to be taken and which reflects the costs as well as the benefits of operating and maintaining the system. Figure 6.2 encapsulates the concept of the logistics information system.

The functions of the logistics information system

A number of specific functions that must be performed by the logistics information system can be identified. These are: a customer service and communications function; a planning and control function and a coordination function (see figure 6.3).

The customer service and communications function

The efficiency with which customer orders are processed and the extent to which communications with customers are maintained is determined by the effectiveness of the logistics information system. The typical logistics system must cope with a wide variety of customer demands. Some customers will order on a regular basis and in standard quantities, e.g. pallet loads. Other customers will order irregularly and for mixed lots. Some will be 'emergency' orders requiring expediting through the system, others may be planned against a predetermined call-off pattern. It is the

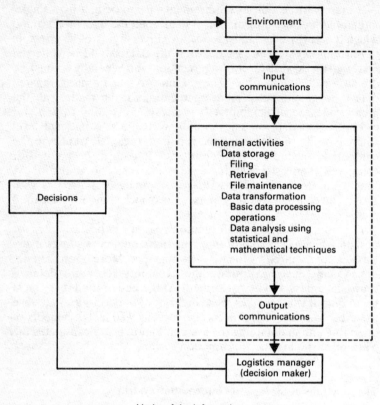

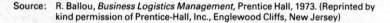
‑‑‑‑‑‑‑‑‑‑‑‑‑ Limits of the information system

Source: R. Ballou, *Business Logistics Management,* Prentice Hall, 1973. (Reprinted by
          kind permission of Prentice-Hall, Inc., Englewood Cliffs, New Jersey)

**Figure 6.2   Elements of the LIS and the relationship to the environment and decision
maker**

supplier's information system which takes the first impact of the
customer's order and thus the system's responsiveness and
flexibility becomes all important.

Equally important is the way in which the information system
provides an adequate communication link between the supplier
and its customers. How easy is it for a customer to establish the
status of an order, for example? Is the customer informed of an
inability to supply through stock-outs or other reasons, or is his
only indication when the goods fail to arrive? One of the most
important aspects of customer service is the maintenance and

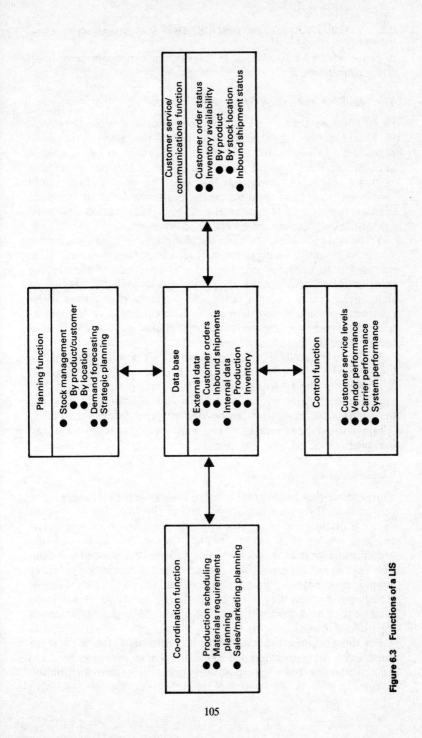

Planning function

- Stock management
  - By product/customer
  - By location
- Demand forecasting
- Strategic planning

Co-ordination function

- Production scheduling
- Materials requirements planning
- Sales/marketing planning

Data base

- External data
  - Customer orders
  - Inbound shipments
- Internal data
  - Production
  - Inventory

Customer service/ communications function

- Customer order status
- Inventory availability
  - By product
  - By stock location
- Inbound shipment status

Control function

- Customer service levels
- Vendor performance
- Carrier performance
- System performance

Figure 6.3 Functions of a LIS

improvement of buyer/supplier relationships through more open communications.

The planning and control function

From what has been said so far the impression might be gained that the function of the logistics information system is simply to react to a customer's order. In fact the system must be capable of anticipating the demands of customers in order that a planned response might be achieved. Likewise the information system should be capable of monitoring the performance of the physical system to identify any variations of actual against planned performance, e.g. service levels, lead times etc.

To provide an adequate basis for planning the logistics information system must incorporate a forecasting facility based upon demand data captured as the order is entered. Obviously the information system is uniquely positioned to perform this task in that order entry is the point of entry to the system. The combination of forecast demand with information on replenishment lead times makes possible the planning of stock and its location within the physical system.

Similarly the control of performance is only possible through the logistics information system. Standards need to be established on all aspects of the logistics system. Thus service levels by product and customer category, as well as facility utilisation targets and budgeted costs, need to be embedded into the system's data base. Against these benchmarks performance can be monitored and variances reported where necessary.

The coordination function

Throughout this book great emphasis has been placed upon the central role of the logistics activity within the company as a means of coordinating the materials flows throughout the system. The concept of logistics stands or falls upon the ability of the organisation to manage its materials flow and the related information flow in an integrated way. Means must therefore be found to enable production planning to be tied in with procurement schedules, for delivery frequencies to be matched to sales-call cycles etc. The common bond that binds these various activities together is shared information.

For this coordination function to be performed effectively there must exist an integrated information system. One writer[1] has suggested a number of prerequisites for an integrated information system:

1   Data entering one subsystem is made available to other subsystems that require it. For example, customer orders entering the order processing system are transformed into computer-readable form and made available for inventory control, production scheduling, sales forecasting etc.

2   Data is consolidated in a common data base to which all interrelated subsystems have access. For instance, in a distribution network with several depots the inventory balance may be held on a central inventory file instead of keeping separate records for each depot.

3   Closely connected activities are consolidated in the same procedure rather than split into separate procedures. For instance, order processing, credit checking and stock allocation are normally performed within the same programme in a computer-based order processing system, whereas in a manual system they are often separated between different departments, e.g. the sales office, the accounting department and the warehouse.

4   A high degree of resource sharing will often take place. For example, the central computer, the data base, the communications network, and the application packages are often shared among all the various subsystems.

The information subsystem

It will be recognised that in reality the logistics information system is not a single system but in fact comprises a number of discrete but linked subsystems.

Figure 6.4 simplifies this notion and suggests two subsystems or 'loops': the supply loop and the customer loop.

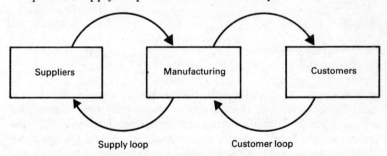

Figure 6.4   Supply and customer loops in the information system

The supply loop

The fundamental purpose of the supply loop is to ensure that raw materials and components are available at the time and place and within the budgeted cost specified by the manufacturing activity. To achieve these objectives data from a number of sources must be collected and integrated. Figure 6.5 shows the inputs and outputs of the supply loop of the logistics information system.

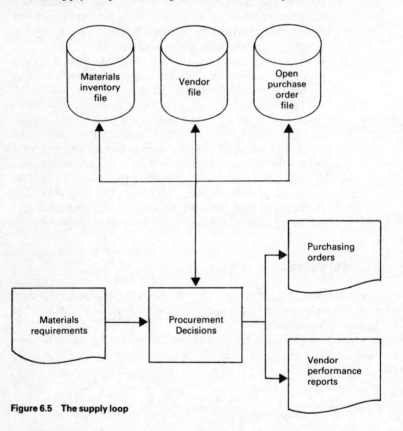

Figure 6.5   The supply loop

The input to the loop is the materials requirements plan specifying the nature, volume and timing of materials, components etc. needed for manufacturing. This must be checked against the inventory on-hand and any orders outstanding. If the need for replenishment is determined a check against the vendor file will identify sources of supply and a purchase order can be generated.

The process itself appears simple and logical, but it must be remembered that a typical company may well deal with many hundreds of suppliers and maintain an inventory of tens of thousands of stockkeeping units. In addition conditions on the supply market must be constantly monitored to warn of potential shortage situations; vendors must be monitored in terms of their supply performance on price, reliability and service. At the same time total on-hand inventory must be kept to a minimum whilst ensuring that manufacturing is never let down! It will be obvious that to keep all these balls in the air the information system must be constantly updated and reporting systems established which will identify potential supply problems before they occur.

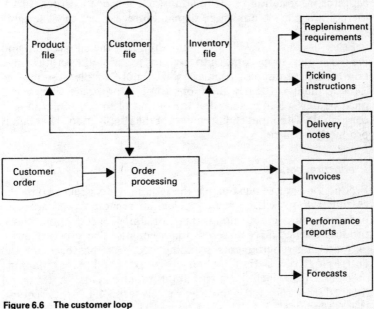

Figure 6.6 The customer loop

The customer loop

In many respects the customer loop is the mirror image of the supply loop (see figure 6.6). Here the customer order is the initiating input to the system. Again the logic is simple but the reality may be more complex. Orders from customers may enter the system at a rate of thousands per day. Each customer's account will have to be examined for creditworthiness, special terms, special requirements etc. The items on the order must then be checked against stock to determine availability. Stock must be allocated to that order and the inventory records updated and replenishment instructions generated if necessary. At the same time picking instructions to the warehouse must be issued, delivery notes raised and invoices generated. Once again it will be realised that all of these activities, whilst capable of manual operation, require the speed and capacity of the computer to ensure the most effective management of the system.

A further output of the customer loop of the logistics information system will be performance reports on such things as achieved service levels, order fill rates, product turnover categories, lead times, damage incidence etc. Also, because the customer loop captures information on demand in the form of the order, this is the point in the system where demand forecasts can most sensibly be generated.

From figure 6.3 it will be remembered that the supply loop and the customer loop come into contact at 'Manufacturing' (in a non-manufacturing environment this is more simply described as 'procurement'). Clearly therefore some appropriate mechanism must be devised to ensure that the output of the customer loop is compatible with input requirements of the supply loop. That link is production control.

Production control

Production control must match the requirements generated by the customer loop with current production schedules and work in progress and, based upon the subsequent production plans, produce a schedule of materials requirements. This process known as materials requirements planning becomes the focus for the entire logistics activity when it is extended as a planning mechanism to include distribution requirements in terms of finished inventory and is more accurately termed 'logistics requirements planning' or LRP (see Chapter 7).

Information technology and the potential for trade-offs

Nowhere has the change in technology been more profound in its effects than in information systems. In logistics management the computer particularly has revolutionised order processing systems for example. It has made possible sophisticated inventory management systems and a host of other applications.

More important than the computer however has been the growth in systems thinking, albeit a product of the computer age, which has made management more aware of the interconnections in the business activity. We now see the importance of taking the total view of things rather than examining just one part of the system. Information, and the technology that makes it available, is the means whereby this total systems thinking becomes possible. Figure 6.7 shows how information from all parts of the business can be related and integrated to give total visibility within the system. These improvements in information flow are obviously not achieved without cost but it is important to recognise that the benefits can be substantial. By improving logistics information systems we should be generating many cost-beneficial trade-offs in the process.

The inventory trade-off

Improvements in order entry and order processing can reduce the total elapsed lead time between the order being placed and the goods being received. Thus the customer need hold less inventory to cover sales during lead time. Furthermore the same benefit is available to the supplier in reducing his own inventory through better production and requirements planning, and reduced customer lead times can improve the company's competitive position. Even if the improvement in lead time is not passed on to the customer in terms of speedier delivery the supplier can make use of the extra time gained to schedule production more efficiently and is less likely to be faced with costly changes to production schedules. This gain can also be reflected in a more consistent lead time to the customer, allowing him to reduce his inventory holding given the greater reliability of supply.

The transport trade-off

Given the extra time for planning as a result of the speed-up in order entry and order processing more efficient use of the transport function can be realised. For example, greater consolidation of loads can be achieved if more time is available for route planning. There will be fewer emergency shipments requiring premium freight and the utilisation of vehicles should improve.

The warehousing trade-off

If information on demand can be fed to the warehouse more quickly then operations at that level can be planned more effectively. However information technology has provided even

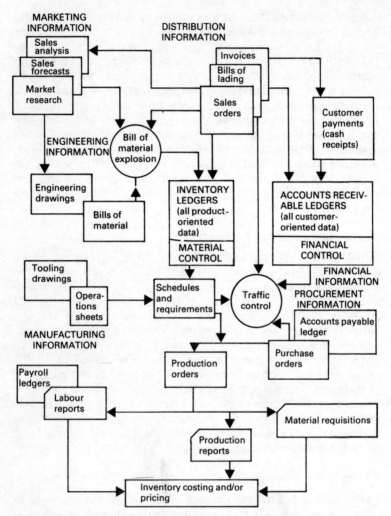

Figure 6.7   The integrated flow of information in the business

greater benefits in warehouse utilisation. The computer can now optimise storage locations for inventory within the warehouse to make maximum use of the space available and to minimise the 'travel' time taken to pick an order. More and more warehouses are using random storage systems which rely on the computer to allocate storage areas and then to instruct the picker on where to pick the items required in a given order. Warehouse productivity can be improved given the more effective use of information, as many companies have found in recent years.

The cash flow trade-off

Perhaps the biggest benefit available through the better use of logistics information is the potential for improved cash flow. Firstly if inventory levels throughout the system can be reduced then working capital is released. Secondly if lead times to the customer are improved then invoices can be issued that much sooner. Many companies still take time to issue an invoice after the goods have been dispatched. Given that the customer will take 30 days or so to pay why add to that payment period by slow invoicing? It is interesting to note in this respect that some companies are currently experimenting with linking their computers with those of their customers' to improve the invoicing process. In the UK for example, Birds Eye Walls Ltd., a frozen food company, is cooperating with Tesco Stores Ltd., one of Britain's major food chains, in an experiment with great potential implications. Tesco receives 100,000 invoices a week from its suppliers and Birds Eye accounts for 2,000 of them. Now the invoices are generated and transmitted electronically by Birds Eye and then cleared for payment by Tesco's computer. It is only a short step from here to a completely integrated system where manufacturers' and retailers' computer systems are linked together from ordering to final payment through electronic funds transfer. The benefits to both parties could be great through the reduction in administrative costs alone. Even bigger pay-offs are available as a result of the improved information on stock positions, demand patterns and order status.

Conclusion

A customer-service oriented logistics system can only operate cost effectively if there is an underlying information system geared to the provision of timely, relevant and accurate information. The design of logistics information systems must parallel the physical flow system and cannot be considered apart from it. In the complex world of fast-changing, highly competitive markets there is an even greater need for responsive logistics systems. Information is the key to that response and technology is the means whereby it is provided. We have deliberately avoided an in-depth investigation of the hardware of technology in this chapter as the rate of change is such that it would be outdated almost as soon as it was written. More important than the technology is an appreciation of the need for a systems approach to logistics information and, unlike the technology, that requirement will not change.

Note

1   T. Skjott-Larsen, 'Integrated Information Systems for Materials Management' in *International Journal of Physical Distribution and Materials Management*, vol. 8, no. 2, 1977.

7   Distribution requirements planning

Prolonged periods of recession in world markets in the 1970s and 1980s have brought about a number of radical changes in business thinking and organisation. One of the most profound effects of high levels of inflation combined with shrinking demand has been the realisation that the resources tied up in manufacturing and distribution systems must be made to work more productively. In earlier chapters great emphasis has been placed upon the need for better deployment of assets in the logistics system and nowhere is the requirement greater than in the use of inventory. High interest rates, themselves a product of macroeconomic responses to recession and inflation, have caused management to reappraise conventional wisdom concerning inventory policy. To make the managerial task even more difficult the financial pressure to reduce inventory levels has had to be reconciled with market pressures for more competitive service levels.

One response to this need to combine lower investment in inventory with maintained or even improved service levels has revolutionised current thinking in this area. The concepts and techniques which have brought about this revolution collectively may be referred to as 'requirements planning' and the implications of this approach for logistics assets management are the subject of this chapter.

New ideas for old

The traditional approach to inventory management is founded upon reorder point and reorder quantity concepts as the basis for determining when to order and in what quantity. Figure 7.1

represents the conventional thinking. Under this approach a reorder point or reorder level is predetermined based upon the expected length of the replenishment lead time. The amount to be ordered may be based upon the economic order quantity (EOQ) formulation which balances the cost of holding inventory against the costs of replacing replenishment orders.

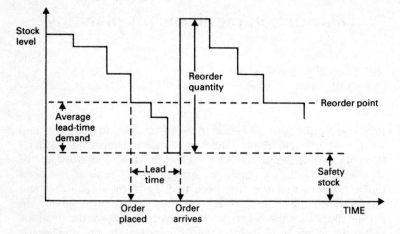

Figure 7.1   The reorder point method of stock control

Alternative methods include the regular review of stock levels with fixed intervals between orders when the amount to be ordered is determined with reference to a predetermined replenishment level as in figure 7.2.

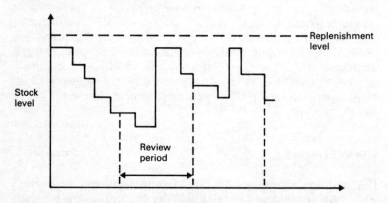

Figure 7.2   A replenishment system based upon periodic review

There are numerous variations on these themes and the techniques have been well documented and practised for many years. However they all tend to share one weakness, that is they frequently lead to stock levels being higher or lower than necessary, particularly in those cases where the rate of demand may change or occurs in discrete 'lumps'. This latter situation frequently occurs when demand for an item is 'dependent' upon demand for another item, e.g. demand for a TV component is dependent upon the demand for TV sets; or where demand is 'derived', e.g. the demand for TV sets at the factory is determined by demand from the retailer which is derived from ultimate demand in the marketplace.

The implications of dependent demand are illustrated in the example given in figure 7.3, which shows how a regular offtake at the retail level can be converted into a much more 'lumpy' demand situation at the plant by the use of reorder points.

A similar situation can occur in a multi-echelon distribution system where the combined demand from each level is aggregated at the next level in the system. Figure 7.4 demonstrates such an occurrence.

The common feature of these examples is that demand at each level in the logistics system is dependent upon the demand at the next level in the system. Demand is termed 'dependent' when it is directly related to, or derives from, the demand for another inventory item or product. Conversely, demand for a given item is termed 'independent' when such demand is unrelated to demand for other items – when it is not a function of demand for other items.[1] This distinction is crucial because whilst independent demand may be forecast using traditional methods, dependent demand must be based upon the demand at the next level in the logistics chain.

Using the example in figure 7.4, it would clearly be inappropriate to attempt to forecast demand at the plant using data based on the pattern of combined demand from the regional centres. Rather it has to be calculated on the identified requirements at each of the preceding levels. It is only at the point of final demand, in this case at the depots, where forecasts can sensibly be made – in fact in most cases demand at the depot would itself be dependent upon retailers' or other intermediaries' demand, but since this is obviously outside the supplier's direct control it is necessary to produce a forecasted estimate of demand. Using the conventional reorder point and economic order quantity approaches to stock control would also be inappropriate in these circumstances because they would not necessarily lead to optimum inventory

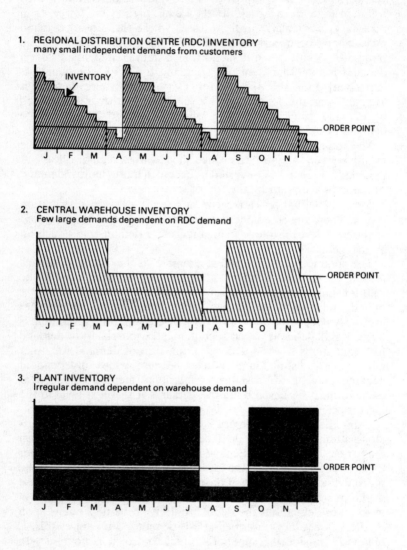

Figure 7.3   Order point and dependent demand

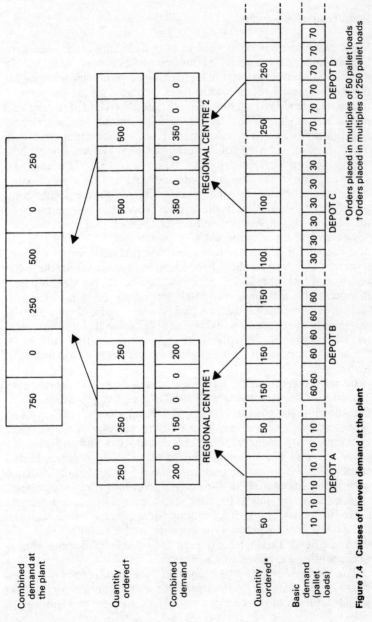

Figure 7.4 Causes of uneven demand at the plant

Combined demand at the plant

| 750 | | 250 | 0 | 500 | 250 | | 0 | 250 |

Quantity ordered†

| | 250 | 250 | | | 500 | | 500 | |

Combined demand

| 200 | 0 | 150 | | | 350 | 0 | 350 | 0 |

REGIONAL CENTRE 1   REGIONAL CENTRE 2

Quantity ordered*

DEPOT A: | | 50 | | 50 |
DEPOT B: | 150 | 150 | 150 | 150 |
DEPOT C: | 100 | 100 |
DEPOT D: | 250 | 250 |

Basic demand (pallet loads)

DEPOT A: | 10 | 10 | 10 | 10 | 10 |
DEPOT B: | 60 60 | 60 | 60 | 60 | 60 |
DEPOT C: | 30 | 30 | 30 | 30 | 30 |
DEPOT D: | 70 | 70 | 70 | 70 | 70 |

*Orders placed in multiples of 50 pallet loads
†Orders placed in multiples of 250 pallet loads

119

levels for the reasons given earlier. What then is the alternative?

Requirements planning

Much attention has been paid in manufacturing management to the concept of 'material requirements planning' (MRP). In essence MRP is a system for forecasting or projecting component part and material requirements from a company's master production schedule (MPS) and the bill of material (BOM) for each end product or module. The time phased requirements for components and materials are then calculated, taking into account stock in hand as well as scheduled receipts. The system establishes, maintains and derives priorities based on regular reviews and updates. One of the key principles of MRP is that it works on a 'time-phased' basis. In other words, the requirements for components are established in the light of when they will be required for production against planned replenishment lead times.

The end result of a successfully implemented MRP system can be a considerably reduced inventory of components and materials, a greater ability to reschedule production to meet changed market needs and a higher level of service in terms of meeting final demand. The techniques of MRP are simple (see, for example, New[2]). However it has only really become practicable through the availability of computer software capable of handling the complexity of information involved in managing multiple products, common components and materials and differing replenishment lead times.

In recent years MRP has been adopted in a wide range of industries. Other methods with similar objectives to MRP originally developed by the Japanese ('Kanban' or 'just-in-time' manufacturing), have also come to be recognised as valuable techniques for reducing on-hand inventory whilst maintaining service levels. The rationale behind these latter methods is that stocks of components or materials should be drastically reduced with replenishment stock for current manufacturing needs being planned to arrive only at the time they are actually needed. Clearly there are considerable implications for suppliers inherent in the use of MRP and Kanban-type approaches by manufacturers, not the least being the increased need for reliable lead times. These issues will be examined in Chapter 8.

The success of the MRP concept has more recently caused distribution planners to consider the opportunities for gaining similar benefits in the distribution activity through the application of the requirements planning logic. This has led to the development of 'distribution requirements planning' (DRP). In a sense DRP is the mirror image of MRP since it seeks to identify requirements for finished product at the point of demand and then produces aggregated, time-phased requirements schedules for each echelon in the distribution system.

DRP is based upon a 'pull' rather than a 'push' philosophy. In other words the emphasis is upon identifying and anticipating customer requirements at the point of demand and this requirement then 'pulls' the product down the distribution pipeline. The alternative is for requirements to be determined centrally and then 'pushed' down the pipeline in accordance with a centrally planned approach to stock allocation.

In a sense many conventional systems are 'pull' systems in that they are reorder point-based, but as we have seen these systems will generally not respond flexibly enough to changed demand requirements. There are arguments in favour of both approaches but generally, if the aim is to meet customer-based service level objectives, it is logical to structure a replenishment system that starts with forecast customer requirements. Furthermore it is highly dangerous to attempt to forecast requirements based solely upon aggregate demand as received at the plant. To refer to the example in figure 7.4, had we tried to forecast requirements based upon the aggregate demand pattern (750, 0, 250, 500, 0, 250) using conventional techniques (say, exponential smoothing) some very odd results would have emerged!

The DRP concept relies upon forecasts of end demand being generated at the lowest point in the distribution echelon, e.g. regional depots, and requirements at each preceding point in the network, e.g. national warehouse and then the plant, are calculated on the basis of aggregations from the levels below, again on a time-phased basis.

Already significant advantages are being demonstrated through the use of DRP,[3,4] but perhaps the biggest pay-off for total systems optimisation is about to happen through the final consummation of the requirements planning logic, i.e. the linking of MRP and DRP into an integrated planning system. Such a link might sensibly be termed 'logistics requirements planning' (LRP).

Figure 7.5 illustrates how LRP combines the logic of DRP and MRP to link the marketplace, through the logistics network, to suppliers. Forecasts of end user requirements on a product-by-product basis are aggregated on a time-phased basis through distribution centres and warehouses to the plant where finished goods requirements are built into a master production schedule which then calculates requirements for components and materials.

What might once have been considered impractical, i.e. the linkage of distribution with manufacturing and ultimately procurement, is now a reality amongst a growing number of firms. Companies like Abbott Laboratories report major improvements in logistics performance involving reduced inventory levels, but with improved customer service through the use of MRP/DRP logic[4] and other similar success stories are beginning to emerge.

LRP in practice

Whilst the concept of requirements planning has an overwhelming logic it is in fact extremely difficult to implement in practice. There are many more companies who have tried to implement it in one form or another and failed than there are who have succeeded.

To make requirements planning work a number of prerequisites exist including: accurate bottom-up forecasts; open lines of communication; flexible manufacturing and distribution systems; improved communications with suppliers and customers. Other necessities include realism in the construction of the master production schedule (MPS), accuracy in the collection of data such as the bill of materials (BOM) and inventory records and, by no means least, a high level of management commitment.

The forecast

As we have seen the basic principle of requirements planning is that it is only independent demand that should be forecast, all other requirements are calculated on the basis of that forecast. In effect this means that the forecast is made at the lowest level in the distribution echelon system. Thus in figure 7.5 the forecast needs to be generated at the local depot level. This 'bottom-up' contrasts with the 'top down' approach which attempts to forecast on the basis of aggregate sales and then allocates forecast demand across depots or regions. There are many dangers with this latter approach, not the least being the 'lumpy' nature of aggregate demand as observed earlier.

This is not to say that 'bottom-up' forecasts are without their problems. Markets may be volatile and the ordering practices of intermediaries, e.g. wholesalers and intermediaries, can distort true end-user demand. Nevertheless the use of sensitive and flexible forecasting procedures of the type discussed in Chapter 9, combined with managerial judgement and 'on-the-ground'

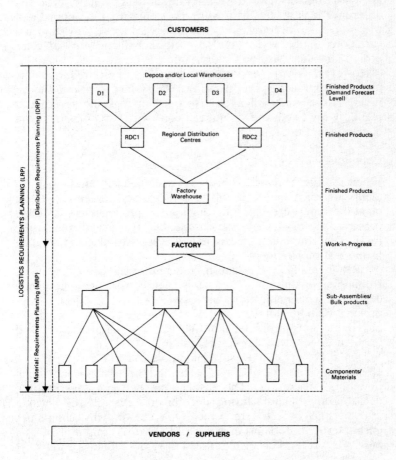

Figure 7.5   Scope of logistics requirements planning

knowledge, is still likely to produce better results when performed as close to the end market as possible.

It should be noted that it is demand that must be forecast rather than sales. This difference is more than semantic. Many information systems capture only data relating to sales rather than demand and base forecasts upon the former rather than the latter. The key difference is that sales data will reflect only what is shipped and will not take account of stock-outs. Likewise any unusual variations in demand caused by seasonal fluctuations or sales promotions must also be factored into the forecast.

However, one of the biggest advantages of the requirements planning approach is that it enables the system to respond more rapidly to demand changes. Thus as long as the forecast is regularly reviewed, the system can cope with variations in actual demand from the forecast level.

Communications

When end-use demand has been forecast and distribution requirements are calculated from this base the combined demand at the plant becomes the input to the master production scheduling process. The master production schedule has a vital role as the focal point for communication between distribution, manufacturing and procurement.

LRP is really a mechanism for improving communications within the organisation, in fact it cannot work without highly developed communications processes. It has the effect of improving 'visibility' all the way down the logistics chain. The impact of requirements at one level in the chain can be quickly assessed for their effect elsewhere in the system.

This more 'open' mode of communication will have profound effects upon the organisation, particularly in terms of individual functional discretion. The distinctions between 'distribution' decisions and 'manufacturing' decisions for example will become blurred and indeed irrelevant. One reason why companies encounter real problems in making LRP work is that it involves a much greater level of organisational integration than is usually the case (see Chapter 10).

System flexibility

Once the safety net of surplus inventory, either in the form of finished goods or components, has been removed and given that end-use demand can never be forecast with 100 per cent accuracy, the logistics system must be capable of rapid response to changed circumstances.

Primarily this flexibility must be available in the manufacturing and distribution subsystems of the firm. Manufacturing particularly must be able to react to production schedules which may change more frequently. This may mean trading off the cost economies of long production runs, albeit with the consequent build up of finished goods inventory, against the benefits of reduced inventory levels through greater flexibility. Recent developments in the area of flexible manufacturing systems using advanced automation techniques and latterly robotics have made it possible in some industries to operate much shorter production runs more economically. At the same time more flexible procedures in the plant, such as group technology, have also contributed to the ability of manufacturing systems to achieve higher service levels on less total inventory in an engineering environment.

A similar flexibility is also required in the distribution subsystem. Thus, providing high levels of customer service without the benefit of large safety stocks means, for example, that vehicle routeing and scheduling must become more responsive to short-term requirements. Similarly the system must be capable of coping with the likely need to increase the number of inter-warehouse movements to balance inventory against requirements. Again recent developments in technology, particularly in computer software, have provided the distribution manager with the means of more rapid response to changed requirements.

Supplier and customer contact

The importance of the forecast in a requirements planning system has already been noted. The forecast can be enhanced if closer relationships with customers, particularly major customers, can be achieved. With greater foreknowledge of customers' requirements planning can be much more precise. A trade-off with the customer – longer lead times for greater reliability – would be ideal. For many customers this is a trade-off they would appreciate. Indeed as customers themselves become more professional as buyers they will demand higher reliability of delivery in order to reduce their own inventory levels. Working more closely with the customer will produce not only a greater visibility of forward requirements but will strengthen the relationship from a marketing point of view.

Similarly it is necessary to establish closer working relationships with suppliers. It is not only the forecast that is crucial to the success of LRP, but also the reliability on the delivery service provided by our suppliers. Procurement decisions are now assuming a much greater importance within the organisation as a whole (see Chapter 8) and one area where this is manifested is in vendor appraisal. Increasingly decisions on sources of supply are based not just on the quality and price of the product but on the reliability of supply. Indeed there is a growing trend towards 'dual' sourcing to ensure a fall-back in case of delivery failure – a fall-back strategy that does not involve the customer in carrying additional stock.

The message therefore is clear: LRP systems are more likely to succeed the closer the relationships between ourselves and our customers on the one hand, and ourselves and our suppliers on the other.

Extending the requirements planning logic

One of the many benefits of a requirements planning system in an organisation is the facility it affords for the planning of resources, e.g. manufacturing capacity, warehouse space, transport facilities etc.

Once the planning system is in place and providing management with forward knowledge of materials and distribution require-ments it follows that bottlenecks and/or redundancies in the system can easily be identified. Many companies with working MRP and DRP systems are now talking about manufacturing resource planning or 'MRP II' systems and distribution resource planning (DRP II) systems which in effect enable physical resource requirements to be planned on a medium to long-term horizon. Thus it is possible to re-examine existing physical facilities to match them more precisely to the streamlined materials flow that is made possible through requirements planning. Adjustments to the system can be made which enable greater utilisation of facilities to be achieved. Combining resource planning with the planning of materials and distribution requirements provides the means for 'closed loop' control of the total logistics system. Figure 7.6 illustrates the logic of this total systems control.

The benefit of this high degree of integration is a better control of materials flow, from components to raw materials through work-in-progress to finished goods, with a resultant reduction in the total investment in inventory. In addition the opportunities for greater utilisation of physical resources such as warehouse space, plant and transportation, means that reductions in fixed logistics assets can be achieved. At the same time the greater flexibility in

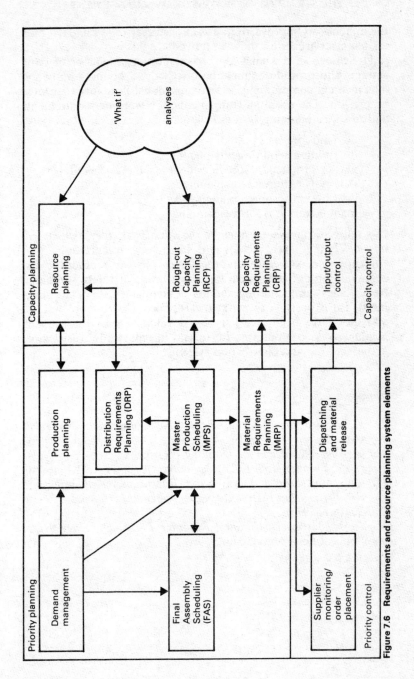

Figure 7.6 Requirements and resource planning system elements

127

the system can improve response to customer requirements, thus enabling service levels to be improved.

To achieve such a high level of integration a number of basic systems and procedures must be installed, to say nothing of the management commitment and organisational flexibility that must be present. The essential components of a working requirements and resource planning system include:

> demand forecasts;
> distribution requirements planning;
> master production schedules/final assembly schedule;
> materials requirements planning;
> distribution resource planning; and
> manufacturing resource planning.

In a sense such a system must be regarded as an 'ideal' which will not be immediately achievable for many organisations that currently use conventional procedures such as reorder points, economic order/batch quantities, high levels of safety stock etc. Nevertheless an increasing number of companies are demonstrating that it is possible to work towards such 'closed-loop' systems and they have been aided in this development by the growing availability of computer software and the move towards flexible manufacturing and distribution systems.

Notes

1   J. R. Orlicky, *Materials Requirements Planning*, McGraw-Hill, 1975.
2   C. New, *Requirements Planning*, Gower, 1973.
3   A. J. Stenger and J. L. Cavinato, 'Adapting MRP to the Outbound Side – Distribution Requirements Planning' in *Production and Inventory Management Journal*, fourth quarter, 1979.
4   A. J. Martin, *Distribution Resource Planning*, Oliver Wight Publications/Prentice Hall, 1983.

8 Distribution and supply channel strategy

Great emphasis has been placed throughout this book on the need to develop a total systems approach to materials and information flow from source to user. The route or routes that these flows may take are the subject of this chapter. Traditionally the 'channel of distribution' is the means whereby products are physically transferred through the system and through which the acquisition transaction takes place. However it is also necessary to recognise the strategic importance of the 'supply channel'. Over and above these considerations is the requirement to place the supply and distribution channel issue into a strategic marketing context. In other words a vital component of an organisation's strategic thinking has to be a clearly defined view on the supply and distribution channel policy it will pursue to achieve its corporate goals.

Many changes are taking place in the supply and distribution environment which can have a radical effect upon the market position of a business. The effect of these changes can often negate an otherwise carefully developed marketing strategy. Most business organisations deal with suppliers and/or buyers which are themselves a part of a chain. Similarly many organisations will not control the entire chain through ownership; they may therefore be faced with a situation where they have a reduced influence on the end user. For example, few manufacturers can control the level of service that a retailer offers the customer on the manufacturer's products – that is a decision determined by the retailer's stocking policy.

The supply and distribution channel can be characterised as a number of intermediaries acting independently of each other and often with conflicting objectives and requirements. Figure 8.1

CHANNEL RELATIONSHIPS

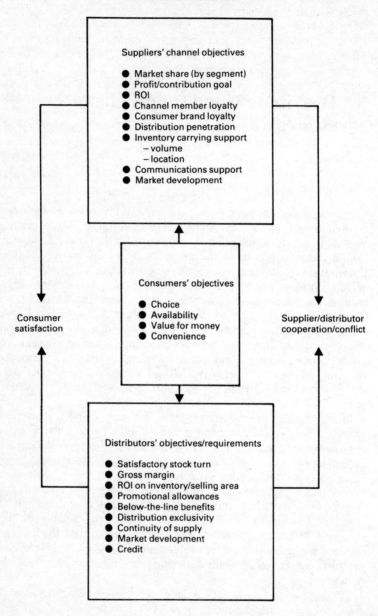

Figure 8.1   Potential for conflict in the channel

shows some of the prime areas of potential conflict between a supplier and a distribution intermediary with the end user sandwiched somewhere in between. Thus, for example, the supplier will probably seek inventory carrying support from his stockist, i.e. a sufficient volume of stock held at the intermediary's premises to meet anticipated demand. On the other hand the intermediary seeks to maximise his return on investment on his total stockholding and therefore seeks to hold minimum inventory but with frequent replenishment.

Problems such as these are common to all buyer/supplier relationships, no matter what type of industry. The basic problem can be categorised as a 'zero-sum game', i.e. a situation where for one party to gain, the other must lose. Thus an increase in profit by, say, a retailer can only come at the expense of the supplier, or the final customer. It need not necessarily be so and the only satisfactory basis for long-run relationships between buyers and suppliers must be one of mutual advantage, a 'non-zero sum game' in fact. There are several ways that such a result can be achieved, but essentially the requirement is for each party in the supply chain to recognise that his output is his customer's input. In other words, improved means need to be found of integrating the logistics connection between buyers and suppliers.

The reasons for the presence of intermediaries in any market is well understood. Alderson[1] writing many years ago succinctly expressed the tasks to be fulfilled within the marketing channel in terms of a number of gaps between production and consumption:

Time gaps Consumers purchase items at more or less discrete intervals, whilst the majority of firms, particularly in the fast-moving consumer goods markets, produce on a continuous basis in order to reap production economies.

Space gaps Consumers are usually dispersed throughout the market; producers are located in a few areas and are often separated by distance from their customers.

Quantity gaps Firms produce large quantities at a time: consumers normally produce in smaller quantities.

Variety gaps The range of products manufactured by a firm is limited; consumers have many needs which require a wide variety of products to satisfy them. To this list Guirdham[2] has added a further 'gap'.

Communications information gap Consumers do not always know the availability and/or the source of the goods they want; producers may not know who and where are the potential purchasers of their products.

These tasks need not be carried out by intermediaries; they can be, and sometimes are, carried out by either the supplier or the buyer. However, it is quite often the case that the most cost effective means of closing these gaps is through the use of channel intermediaries such as agents, jobbers, distributors, wholesalers, retailers etc. Put very simply, the use of an intermediary becomes appropriate when the cost of closing one of the gaps above is greater without one than with one. This is demonstrated in figure 8.2 where five producers are selling to five end users. Without an intermediary there are twenty-five sets of physical and trans-actional links; with an intermediary this is reduced to ten. Whilst this is an over-simplification it highlights the principle of the efficient marketing channel.

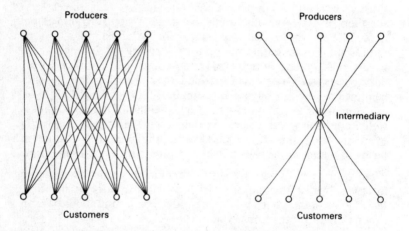

Figure 8.2   The effect of an intermediary in the marketing channel

However it is not only cost considerations that have to be weighed in the decision to utilise intermediaries in the channel. Of equal importance is the impact on the supplier's marketing effectiveness. The problem here is that the marketing objectives of the supplier may not coincide with those of the intermediary. The intermediary may well be acting for other suppliers too and his priorities and loyalties may be divided.

The benefits of using intermediaries must be balanced carefully against the costs. Some of the benefits include better coverage, lower selling costs, wider product range, customer convenience, market knowledge and customer finance, while among the costs are loss of margin, loss of marketing control, low priority given and inadequate customer service.

One way to view this problem is to think in terms of a product's final 'added value', i.e. its final end-user selling price less the cost to the producing firm of its bought in materials and supplies. How much of that total added value should the firm be prepared to trade-off by way of margins and discounts to intermediaries in return for assistance in closing the production-consumption gaps identified earlier?

At the outset of this chapter it was argued that the organisation must look in both directions when formulating its channel strategy: backwards to its suppliers and forwards to its customers. Whilst supply strategy and market strategy are highly connected, it is convenient to consider each in turn and then to seek an integration at the conclusion.

Supply channel strategy

Changes in the marketing environment come from all directions. The firm, in its anxiety to focus its efforts upon the marketplace, will often neglect to observe the changes that may be occurring on the supply side. A strategy for supply is just as important as a market strategy.

The impact of supply factors on profit is not always fully realised; for example, one British automobile manufacturer has identified that its total purchasing budget when expressed as a percentage of its sales turnover is 60 per cent. In manufacturing industry generally, the cost of bought-in materials and services commonly accounts for over 50 per cent of sales turnover.[3] With the usual low profit margins in many of these businesses even 1 or 2 per cent saving can have dramatic effects on profitability.

Further problems in the supply environment can come from the lack of certainty over future availability of materials. Many basic materials will one day be exhausted and substitutes will need to be planned for. More importantly in some cases, but less often realised, many industries are dependent to a greater or lesser extent upon materials which are only available from a very limited number of suppliers or geographical areas. These are the so-called 'strategic materials' where in effect the control of availability is in the hands of a few suppliers. For example, the UK is highly dependent on overseas suppliers for a number of vital metals, particularly chromium, cobalt, tungsten, manganese, vanadium, molybdenum, niobium and platinum.

The vulnerability of manufacturers using these materials is made worse by the fact that the major sources of supply are often based in politically unstable countries, or countries that may not always be prepared to supply the UK. For example, South Africa and neighbouring Zimbabwe hold 97 per cent of known resources of chromium. South Africa and the Soviet Union between them account for 80 per cent of all manganese reserves, 92 per cent of vanadium and 98 per cent of the platinum group of metals. In the case of molybdenum, a vital ingredient of some high-performance steel alloys, and niobium, another irreplaceable alloying element, the vulnerable sources of supply are in South America. Two-thirds of the world's demand for niobium is met by just one mining company in Brazil!

Competition for scarce minerals and metals is on the increase with the growth of new industrial nations. This combined with the increased sophistication of suppliers in bargaining and the use of cartels, OPEC being perhaps the best known example, means that the supply environment for many companies can only become more uncertain.

Some questions raised by these changes in the supply environment must be addressed in an attempt to develop a strategy for supply:[4]

1   Will constraints in raw materials availability jeopardise achievement of growth objectives?
2   How will raw material price changes affect profitability objectives?
3   Should resources be diverted from opportunities for growth to protection of supply?
4   Can new products now under development go into production? Will cost targets be met?
5   Will changes in materials quality affect manufacturing efficiency or end-product quantity?

The appropriate corporate response to these questions will differ according to situation, but there will be major implications for the supply channel and the logistics of maintaining that supply. Some companies have been vigorously pursuing a strategy of 'backwards integration', that is buying into their sources of supply. Many of the world's petro-chemical producers have been pursuing this strategy whilst also diversifying their feedstock sources. For example, the purchase by DuPont of Conoco has given DuPont access to both coal and oil-based feedstock sources.

At a less global level other companies have found that

backwards integration can smooth logistical planning. The great increase in the sales of Perrier Water, for example, in the last ten years has been aided considerably by the total production and logistical integration that exists with the company manufacturing its own bottles from its own raw materials and filling them with its own water!

Backwards integration can be achieved by means other than ownership, however, with equally satisfactory results. Marks and Spencer does not own its suppliers but has developed the closest possible working relationship with them, in which M & S managers are actively involved with suppliers in product planning/quality control and logistics management.

It can be argued that to achieve supply integration without actual ownership is more desirable than integration through ownership, with all the consequent problems and lack of flexibility that such a strategy can bring.

Volvo's supply strategy

As an example of how a manufacturer can achieve a high degree of integration without owning its suppliers and at the same time improve its logistical operations, let us take the case of Volvo,[5] the Swedish car manufacturer, in its European operations.

Nearly three-quarters of every Volvo car is made outside Sweden, thus placing a considerable requirement on both supplier relations and the management of the supply network. Volvo places tight replenishment demands upon its suppliers, but it has also invested in its own logistics systems to develop a situation where all parties are better off. In particular it has developed a purchasing strategy of 'ex-works buying'. In other words it pays its suppliers for the goods less delivery costs and Volvo arranges its own collection and shipping. Thus in the UK components are collected by a transport operator, contracted by Volvo, on a pre-planned basis and taken to a central warehouse at Immingham for storage before shipment to Gothenberg in Sweden. One of the important features of this system is that the cost of holding the stock, including the warehousing, is not borne by Volvo – it only pays for items when they are withdrawn from stock. Currently as a condition of purchase suppliers must be prepared to maintain between two and four weeks' stock of components to Immingham. Suppliers must also use standardised crates and pallets supplied by Volvo and use Volvo's special identification labels on those crates. A crate will normally not be opened until it arrives at the assembly line. Thus quality control also becomes the responsibility of the supplier.

This places substantial demands upon suppliers, but in return Volvo works closely with its suppliers in communicating its requirement as far in advance as possible. Volvo tries to make its projections as close to firm orders as possible, using short, medium, and long-term estimates. Most suppliers find Volvo's estimates to be accurate[6] and can base their own production schedules around them. The Volvo scheduling system is based on a twelve-month rolling forecast, of which the first six weeks constitute a firm order; the next three months form a period in which Volvo is responsible for raw materials and work-in-process in the firms, but in which Volvo is free to vary its requirements; the rest of the twelve months' projection is tentative.

The success of this strategy is reflected in Volvo's steady reduction in the real costs of production and logistics on the one hand and the greater ability of its suppliers to plan and manage their own operations.

In many ways this example typifies the increased reliance that manufacturers are placing upon suppliers as they adopt the 'Kanban' or 'just-in-time' manufacturing systems referred to in Chapter 7. There is now an even greater need for buyers and suppliers to work more closely together and to coordinate their logistics operations. The results of such coordination invariably lead to improved profitability for both parties.

Marketing channel strategy

In just the same way that the supply environment has changed for many companies, so too has the market environment and in particular the nature of the distribution channels open to these companies. Some dramatic changes in distribution channels have taken place with great implications for companies competing in those markets; consider, for example, the growth of retail outlets for computers, for business as well as home use, in response to the reduction of the real price of computers relative to traditional methods of selling and distribution. Who would have thought ten years ago that IBM would be using retail channels of distribution? Similarly the meteoric rise of Sinclair Computers in the UK was due in part to innovative distribution, in the first place through the use of mail order and secondly through high-street multiples.

In the past most companies did not see the channel of distribution as being a variable in their marketing mix, but now it is increasingly vital for an organisation to review constantly its strategy towards its channels.

In some cases this force for change has come about as a result of pressure from channel intermediaries. Consider, for example, the changes in the UK retailing scene over the last twenty or so years and, in particular, the changes in packaged food distribution. From being a 'nation of shopkeepers' with grocery stores on almost every corner there now exists one of the most concentrated grocery markets in the world. Currently just three retail organisations account for 40 per cent of packaged groceries purchased in the UK. Clearly this means that substantial power is held by the major grocery retailers – companies like Tesco, Sainsbury and Asda. This power is manifested not only in the retailers' ability to drive the manufacturers' price down to ever lower levels, but also in their ability to specify service levels, delivery frequency, method of delivery, pallet type etc.

This shift in the balance of power has led to reappraisals of marketing strategy by manufacturers which more often than not have been belated reactions, rather than a pro-active search for alternative distribution strategies. For this reason greater cooperation is necessary between supplier and distributor as the only ultimate way of achieving a mutually satisfactory relationship in the marketing channel.

Firstly, it would be appropriate to identify the factors to be taken into account when attempting to develop a marketing channel strategy. At the outset it must be recognised that channel strategy has to be an integral part of a firm's marketing strategy. In other words overall marketing objectives need to be clearly defined, target markets delineated and a brand positioning strategy developed. Only then can rational decisions on channel strategy be made. At the same time the customers' requirements must be considered. Do they seek value for money primarily, or convenience, or availability, or are they motivated in the choice of purchase point by 'identity', i.e. relating the outlet to their own personality or even life style? Whilst these factors relate particularly to consumer markets, similar questions must be asked in industrial marketing contexts – channel strategy is just as relevant to a company such as Castrol in the distribution of specialised industrial cutting oils as it is to the distribution of GTX, their major consumer brand of motor oil.

The decisions involved in the development of a channel strategy can be examined from two points of view: channel length and channel breadth.

Channel length

Channel length concerns the extent to which intermediaries should be used or, at the other extreme, whether sales should be made directly to the consumer. This decision is not just a question of economics but should be governed by the extent to which the firm is prepared to trade-off control of the marketing channel to intermediaries.

If intermediaries are used there are three options available, all differing in the degree of channel control retained by the firm. The first is to construct a corporate system, in which the manufacturer owns and operates a vertically integrated, 'captive' channel system. For example, HMV owns a chain of retail record stores, or the major brewers own tied public houses. The main problem with this type of 'vertical marketing system' is that the manufacturer may not have the necessary strengths to move into what is quite a different business area. In earlier times Cyril Lord tried to extend from manufacturing carpets into retailing with disastrous consequences. Currently Xerox is having a difficult time trying to succeed with its own office equipment retail stores.

The second option is the contractual system. The most common manifestation of this is franchising, one of the fastest growing sectors in distribution today. Franchise arrangements can be of two forms: 'product trade-name franchising' and 'business format franchising'. The former consists primarily of product distribution arrangements in which the franchisee acquires the right to market the franchising product within a designated market area using the franchiser's trade name. Main car dealers are an example of this type of arrangement. Business format franchising consists of more integrated arrangements in which the franchisee acquires the right to offer the franchiser's product or services in a designated market area, but in addition must adopt the trading 'format' laid down by the franchiser, e.g. physical fittings, procedures, quality control etc. Many of today's 'fast food' chains operate on this principle, e.g. Kentucky Fried Chicken, and Wimpy. It is also found in other business areas such as hotels (Holiday Inns), car hire (Hertz) and printing (Prontaprint). The advantage to the franchiser is that it allows for increased market coverage whilst still maintaining control over the channel of distribution.

The third option is the conventional channel system employing independent intermediaries such as agents, wholesalers and retailers. These are by far the most widespread and, whilst being the most easily accessible from the suppliers' point of view, they present problems of control. Nevertheless they still offer many opportunities for profitable business expansion through cooperation. There are signs in some industries that manufacturers and intermediaries are working more closely together to develop a form of marketing 'symbiosis' whereby the total performance of the entire channel is improved by coordinated marketing and distribution programmes. This can take many forms from co-operation in new product development to linked information systems for ordering and invoicing. Indeed we are probably only just beginning to appreciate the opportunities that exist for such cooperation and hence for mutual profit improvement.

The major justification for conventional channels is that they are based upon a concept of specialisation whereby manufacturers and intermediaries concentrate on what they do best. One development which reflects this has been the considerable growth of so-called 'third party operations'. These companies are usually distribution specialists who offer a range of services and merchandising support. Companies such as SPD, TLT Transport, Lowfields, BRS, and others have developed significant businesses in the last fifteen years. In other cases manufacturers have 'hived-off' their entire distribution activity and have concentrated on manufacturing and marketing. A recent example of this was the decision of Whitbreads, one of the major brewers in the UK, to set up a joint company with the National Freight Corporation to handle its entire retail distribution.

Channel breadth

The decision on channel breadth is essentially one of market coverage. At the extremes are 'intensive' distribution and 'selective' distribution. An example of a product intensively distributed would be the ubiquitous Mars Bar, which can be purchased at newsagents, supermarkets, works canteens and even garages. In markets such as confectionery wide distribution is essential to market share which is closely correlated to profitability. On the other hand the would-be purchaser of a Bang and Olufsen hi-fi has to search out the authorised stockist. In this case the manufacturer has deliberately restricted its availability both for marketing and product support reasons.

The decision to seek intensive or selective distribution will be influenced by product characteristics, buyer behaviour, the degree of channel control desired and the overall marketing strategy.

Product characteristics refer to the extent to which a product is a 'convenience' item, i.e. one that customers frequently purchase and seek the minimum of effort in acquiring, e.g. soft drinks; or, at the other extreme, where the product is a 'speciality' item, e.g. hi-fi, where the customer may be expected to 'shop around'.

Buyer behaviour will affect the channel decision to the extent that where perceived risk is high and where information is sought prior to purchasing, or alternatively where brand loyalty may be high, or the customer seeks 'individuality' in a product, then selective distribution will generally be more appropriate.

Degree of control which a supplier can exert over a channel is likely to be higher in a selective distribution system than an intensive system.

Marketing strategy should be a major determinant of channel breadth. If a high level of distribution coverage is required to generate market share then intensive distribution is more likely to achieve it. On the other hand the marketing strategy may be geared in part to a certain level of 'exclusivity', say designer jeans or cosmetics. In this case intensive distribution would tend to negate the overall marketing strategy. It is often the case that products move from selective to intensive distribution as they move through their life cycle. The decision as to what is an appropriate distribution strategy and what is not must ultimately be linked to the marketing objectives for the product and the business. Only when this is recognised can a coherent distribution channel strategy be achieved.

Assessing marketing channel effectiveness

If the marketing channel is to be managed more effectively, a means of monitoring the performance of intermediaries must be found. Surprisingly, few organisations formally measure the cost-effectiveness of their marketing channels. As a result many opportunities for profit improvement are missed; these opportunities may arise through possible reductions in channel costs and/or through improvements in sales performance.

A practical framework for the evaluation of marketing channel effectiveness is the strategic profit model.[7] As figure 8.3 illustrates, it is possible to use this model to examine both the current profit performance of a marketing channel and also to identify the change in return on investment resulting from any variation in channel performance. For example, the effect of reducing the number of intermediaries in favour of fewer, larger ones can be estimated. In this case it might be seen that transport costs

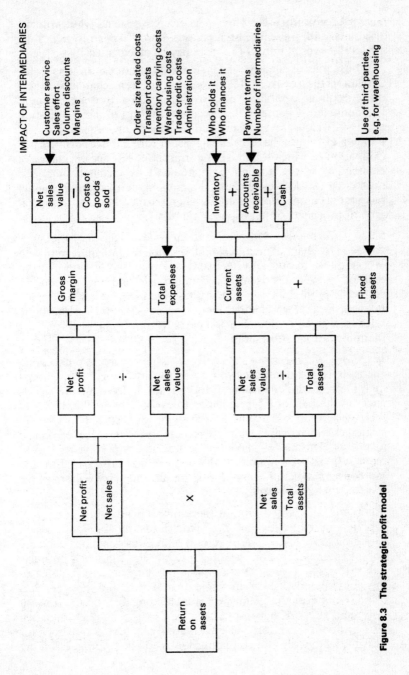

Figure 8.3   The strategic profit model

141

decrease, inventory carrying costs decrease slightly but volume discounts and trade credit increase. Using the strategic profit model the overall impact of this policy change can easily be seen.

Whilst this evaluative framework is strategic in its focus, indicating the relative effectiveness of different channels, other, more frequent, appraisals of current channel performance should be conducted. Chapter 5 discussed the concept of the distribution audit in which the channel audit formed an integral part. A number of criteria have been suggested for channel performance evaluation of which the most important are: sales performance of channel members; inventory maintained by channel members; marketing capabilities of channel members; motivation of channel members; competition faced by channel members, and general growth prospects of the channel members.[8]

Sales performance   Obviously at the end of the day the sales achieved by channel members on the supplier's behalf have to be a crucial measure of their effectiveness. However it is vital that the cost of those sales is also accounted for and the concept of customer profitability analysis as described in Chapter 4 is highly relevant here. Two channel members may account for the same sales in a given period, but the costs to the supplier of servicing them may differ substantially.

Inventory maintenance   A current issue in many marketing channels is the question 'who holds the inventory?'. In today's high interest rate environment there is an understandable reluctance on the part of intermediaries to carry large stockholdings at their cost. Increasingly the search is on for distribution channel strategies which enable higher levels of sales to be achieved on less inventory. This means that more flexible and responsive replenishment systems are required or that the supplier is prepared to ship 'on consignment', in other words the intermediary only pays for the stock when it is sold.

Marketing capability   One of the important attributes sought by suppliers in their choice of intermediaries is the ability to take on to a greater or lesser extent certain marketing functions. Usually one of the key functions would be selling the supplier's products either through a sales force or some other means. In some cases this could be undertaken in whole or in part by the supplier, thus using the intermediary only as a stockholding distributor. It is not only sales support that would be sought by the supplier but often also promotional effort. The marketing channel is not only for distribution but also for communications and the willingness of the intermediary to promote actively the supplier's products is of considerable importance.

Motivation of channel members   There is a vast literature on the determinants of cooperation and conflict in the marketing channel (see, for example,[8]). The basic problem is one of interorganisational relations and the relative balance of power in the channel. Because intermediaries have different objectives from suppliers, this often tends to lead to an adversarial type of relationship. The UK grocery market in the recent past has been characterised by this type of conflict between the major retailers and the manufacturers who supply them. There are signs that this situation is changing with a greater recognition than cooperation can produce rewards for both parties.

Competition in the channel   Competition within the channel can be of two types: between intermediaries, for example one retailer against another; and within an intermediary with similar products. The first type of competition is more of a threat if the supplier is pursuing a strategy of selective distribution – he will be more vulnerable to shifts in the share of the market controlled by competing intermediaries. A supplier must endeavour not to become 'locked-in' through exclusive distribution agreements when there is the prospect of major shifts in the competitive structure amongst intermediaries.

The second form of competition will occur whenever the intermediary also handles substitute products. In some distributive contexts this can be avoided through 'solus' type agreements where the intermediary agrees not to carry competing lines. More often than not, however, a supplier will find that competition within an intermediary is an important factor to be considered. At the retail level this competition manifests itself in the form of the 'fight for shelf space' in which a product competes not only with substitutes but with all the other lines carried by the retailer.

Growth prospects   One large UK company supplying garden tools had always had a strong presence in hardware outlets and specialist tool shops. However, it had neglected to observe the emergence of new type outlets such as garden centres and the larger do-it-yourself stores. At the same time the hardware store was in decline. As a result of this and other factors it suffered a substantial loss of market share.

This example illustrates the importance of understanding the dynamics of marketing channels in developing long-term strategies for distribution. The success of a supplier in the end is closely connected to the success of its intermediaries.

The theme of this chapter has been the importance of supply and distribution channel decisions upon the marketing success of the business. The logistics concept recognises the interrelationship of supply and distribution but only rarely are they managed as an entity. Sufficient evidence exists however to confirm the benefits that are available through more vigorous management of these channels. In many businesses 'channel management', although neglected, is crucial to longer-term profitability. Naturally organisational issues are raised in considering how to manage better the supply and distribution channels and these will be considered in Chapter 10. However, more important are the implications for the management of relationships with suppliers and distributors. The basic prerequisite for improved marketing channel effectiveness is the establishment of a 'channel culture' based upon cooperation rather than conflict – put another way, a 'non-zero-sum game'.

Notes

1   W. Alderson, 'Factors governing the development of marketing channels' in Richard M. Clewett (ed), *Marketing Channels for Manufactured Products*, Richard D. Irwin, 1954.

2   M. Guirdham, *Marketing: the Management of Distribution Channels*, Pergamon Press, 1972.

3   L. W. Stern and A. I. El-Ansary, *Marketing Channels*, Prentice Hall, 1977.

4   M. D. Webber, 'Strategic Raw Materials Planning' in *Proceedings of the 1981 International Logistics Conference*, San Francisco, 1981.

5   'Volvo squeezes the components pipeline' in *International Management*, March 1983.

6   'Volvo's Component Pipeline' in *Materials Handling News*, April 1977.

7   Bowersox *et al.*, *Management in Marketing Channels*, McGraw Hill, 1980.

8   R. Pegram, *Selecting and Evaluating Distributors*, National Industrial Conference Board, New York, 1965.

9 Developing the distribution plan

Many companies have recognised the need to develop more formal approaches to planning. The uncertainties of the market environment and the increased complexity of business decisions have provided an incentive to these organisations to seek ways in which corporate resources can be better allocated and contingencies provided for. Nevertheless formal business planning still tends to be confined to the larger companies, and often those that are involved in so-called fast-moving markets. Thus the Unilevers and Proctor & Gambles of the world are using highly sophisticated planning techniques, while many other companies still lag behind. This is due not so much to a lack of resources to commit to the planning function, but more often to a lack of appreciation of the necessity for planning.

Planning enables the business to anticipate change rather than to react to it. It also assists in the identification of risk and enables the costs and benefits of alternative strategies to be more precisely assessed. Without a planning orientation the organisation is simply carried along by the tide of events rather than actually influencing the shape of those events.

This chapter is concerned primarily with distribution planning but it is important to recognise its relationship to the other planning activities of the business. In the hierarchy of planning concepts, the distribution plan is a subset of the marketing planning function which is itself given direction by the corporate plan.

The corporate plan is a statement of the overall business strategy detailing the definition of the business, the global corporate missions, the directions for future development and resource allocation and the specification of financial objectives for the firm. Once these overall business objectives are determined the way becomes clearer for the development of the marketing plan specifying how those corporate requirements will be achieved through the sale of products, or services, into markets. The marketing plan itself comprises four major components, each reflecting the key elements of the marketing mix: product, pricing, promotion and distribution. Here we focus on the distribution plan, but it must be recognised that no one element of the marketing mix can be considered in isolation. Hence in developing the distribution plan constant cross-reference must be made to its interrelationship with the other marketing mix elements.

Distribution planning horizons

Distribution planning has to work both at the short-term and the long-term levels. Short-term or 'operational' planning will normally extend for a budget or calendar year, while a longer-term view, perhaps with a horizon of five or more years, might be termed 'strategic' or 'resource' planning.

Operational planning, as its title suggests, is concerned with the planning of appropriate responses to events, whilst resources are fixed, to all intents and purposes. It is in reality the planning of the day-to-day management of the system. Operational planning is concerned with such issues as vehicle scheduling, lead-times, inventory replenishment, warehouse utilisation etc. This has often been the area of 'seat of the pants' management, usually followed by 'firefighting'. Now with the advent of more systematic management and planning concepts, a greater discipline is being exerted in this area. The impact that 'decision support systems' can have upon the development of better operational planning will be discussed later.

Strategic planning is concerned with the longer-term allocation of resources and adopts a time-frame where all resources are variable. Issues such as the number and location of depots, changes in transport mode and new channels of distribution are the types of decisions affected at this level of planning. The strategic role of distribution is often neglected and yet, as we have seen in earlier chapters, the ability to respond effectively to market and environmental changes is just as necessary in distribution as it is elsewhere in the business. The penalties for neglecting the strategic component of the distribution task are usually expensive, e.g. a depot network unsuited to current market requirements and current cost profiles or commitment to distribution modes that do not meet changed criteria for cost effectiveness.

The distribution planning framework

There are many tasks to be encompassed within the distribution planning framework. The first is to gain a detailed understanding of the present position. This is the distribution audit that was described in Chapter 5. Without this comprehensive picture of the present operating characteristics and capabilities of the business it is impossible to move on to the setting of distribution missions and objectives. The definition of missions and objectives is a vital step in the planning process. In the words of the old saying, 'If we don't know where we're going, any road will take us there!'. The concept of the distribution mission was introduced briefly in Chapter 4 where it was defined as 'a set of goals to be achieved by the system within a specific product/market context'.

Missions can be defined in terms of the type of channels and outlets served, by the products that are sold to them within the constraints of specified levels of cost and service. Figure 9.1 highlights some of the factors that could be relevant in the definition of distribution missions.

The importance of this stage of the process is that it provides the focus for subsequent decisions. Naturally the precise definition of distribution missions and the specific objectives that flow from that definition will need to be based upon marketing and operational requirements and hence the need for the fullest coordination at the planning level between these different areas. As a result of the careful specification of missions and objectives the next stage in the planning sequence can follow logically, that is the development of distribution strategies.

Strategies are the means whereby objectives are to be achieved – the 'route to the goal'. Normally there will be alternative strategic options available to the business in its pursuit of objectives and one of the tasks of planning is to identify and evaluate them. In the case of distribution strategy, the planner will be concerned to examine options in terms of cost effectiveness. This can either mean seeking strategies that will achieve required customer service objectives at least cost, or working within a given distribution budget and attempting to maximise service. Whilst the former may be the more desired approach, the latter is often adopted for pragmatic reasons.

Murray[1] has summarised the distribution planning process as follows:

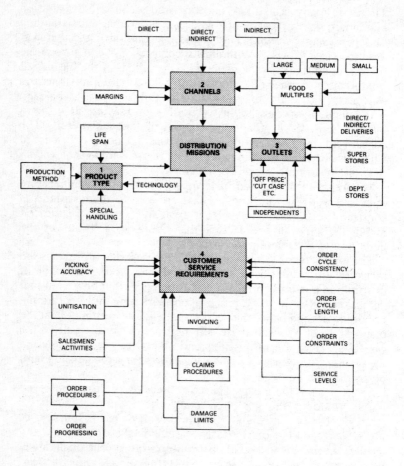

Figure 9.1 Defining distribution missions

1   Developing a thorough understanding and appreciation of business strategies and marketing plans. This understanding is essential for providing sound strategic planning recommendations and for moving toward a distribution system that balances cost and service effectiveness.

2   Evaluating customer service requirements to determine what elements are viewed as key – how service is measured, and what levels of performance are expected, and how the business measures up against its competition.

3   Analysing the distribution system and total costs of production/distribution to identify the lowest cost network that meets business marketing and customer requirements.

Thus the basis for the development of viable distribution strategies rests upon the recognition of customer service requirements and the costs of providing that service combined with an understanding of global corporate goals.

Based upon these principles we can construct a distribution plan which indicates the linkages from corporate objectives down to the specific components of distribution strategy. The plan should include sections on corporate objectives, marketing strategies and customer service strategies as well as specific detail on inventory, warehousing, transport and customer communications strategy. These latter aspects represent the core of the distribution plan, both at the strategic and the operational level, and the plan should cover at least the following:

Inventory strategy which includes service level policy, replenishment strategy, differential deployment (ABC concept), stock-turn targets and stock location.

Warehousing strategy comprising the number of stockholding points, location of depots, use of public warehouses, warehouse design and layout and materials handling methods.

Transport strategy comprising own account/third party split, lease/buy decisions, customer pick-up/direct delivery/other options, vehicle utilisation targets, routeing flexibility and modal split.

Customer communications strategy comprising order cycle time policy, differential customer response strategies, order processing systems, damages/claims/returns strategy and order status reporting.

The final planning task is the development of monitoring and control procedures. It will be obvious that planning and implementation will come to nothing without an efficient means of monitoring and controlling the 'actual' against the 'plan'.

A suitable focus for such a monitoring system is customer service, both from the view of performance and the costs of its provision. Setting up the service monitor should be a systematic procedure. Heskett et al.[2] suggest a sequence which, slightly modified, would be:

1   Identify all important logistics cost categories along with other inputs of effort which the organisation incurs in providing customer service.
2   Institute systems and procedures for the collection of this cost data.
3   Identify and collect output data.
4   Prepare a set of desired measures by which the logistics activities within the organisation might be evaluated.
5   Set up a mechanism for the regular presentation of status reports.

This procedure begins with the recognition that customer service costs, wherever they occur, should be flushed out and brought together. Usually traditional accounting systems will not be capable of providing the data in the form in which it is required. Many customer service costs will be lost in the 'general overheads' of the business, e.g. order processing costs. Designing the procedures for the collection of this data is therefore no easy task.

Identifying and collecting output data may also be problematic. Output data in the customer service context is concerned with revenue, thus the problem becomes one of pinpointing the extent to which the service package has resulted in the generation of revenue. Obviously this is not possible and so, assuming a relationship between revenue generation and service level, the latter is used as a surrogate measure. Hence measures such as order cycle time, percentage of back orders, consistency of delivery lead-times etc. have to be used. Fairly simple recording and reporting systems will normally be sufficient to generate the required data. For example, regular samples can be taken of individual customer orders to check on order cycle lead-times, likewise for the percentage of orders met from stock.

Measuring performance within the logistics organisation involves the collection, on the same regular basis, of such data as the cost of warehousing (handling, storage) and utilisation, transportation and utilisation, inventory, order processing etc. This data is often conveniently presented in the form of ratios, e.g. cost per case, cost per ton-mile etc.

The reporting format of such a customer service monitoring system will vary according to the requirements of the individual company. Ballou[3] gives an example of what such a periodic customer service control statement could look like (see table 9.1). Information such as this should be compared with the performance standards previously set. As far as cost standards are concerned, some care is necessary in setting these standards. In Chapter 5, mention was made of the need to adopt a flexible budgeting

Table 9.1
Periodic customer service statement

Physical distribution

Transportation of finished goods:

freight charges inbound to warehouse	$2,700,000	
delivery charges outbound from warehouses	3,150,000	
freight charges on stock returns to plant	300,000	
extra delivery charges on back orders	450,000	
		$6,600,000

Finished goods inventories:

inventories in transit	280,000	
storage costs at warehouse (*a*)	1,200,000	
materials-handling costs at warehouse	1,800,000	
cost of obsolete stock	310,000	
storage costs at plant (*a*)	470,000	
materials-handling costs at plant	520,000	
		4,580,000

(Table 9.1 continued)

Order-processing costs:

processing of customer orders	830,000	
processing of stock orders	170,000	
processing of backorders	440,000	
		1,440,000

Administration and overhead – finished goods:

proration of unallocated managerial expenses	240,000	
depreciation of owned storage space	180,000	
depreciation of materials-handling equipment	100,000	
depreciation of transportation equipment	50,000	
		570,000
Total distribution costs		$13,190,000

Physical supply

Transportation of supply goods:

freight charges inbound to plant	$1,200,000	
expedited freight charges	300,000	
		1,500,000

Supply goods inventories:

storage costs of raw materials	300,000	
materials-handling cost on raw materials	270,000	
		570,000

Order processing:

processing of supply orders	55,000	
costs of expedited orders	10,000	
		65,000

(Table 9.1 concluded)

Administration and overhead – supply goods: proration of unallocated managerial expenses	50,000	
depreciation of owned storage space	30,000	
depreciation of materials-handling equipment	40,000	
depreciation of transportation equipment	25,000	
Total supply costs		$2,280,000
Total distribution costs		$13, 190,000
Total logistics costs		$15,470,000

Customer service

Percentage of warehouse deliveries within one day	92%
Average in-stock percentage (*b*)	87%
Total order cycle time (*c*)	
Normal processing	7 ± 2 days
Back order processing	10 ± 3 days
Backorders	
Total	503
Percentage of total orders	2.5%
Customer returns due to damage, dead stock, order-processing and late deliveries (*d*)	1.2%
Percentage of available production time shut-down due to supply stockouts	2.3%

(*a*) Includes space, insurance, taxes and capital costs.
(*b*) Percentage of individual product items filled directly from warehouse stocks.
(*c*) Based on distribution of order cycle times.
(*d*) Percentage of gross sales.

Source: R. Ballou, *Business Logistics Management*, Prentice Hall, 1973. (Reprinted with permission)

concept where account is taken of the changed level of activity or volume and the effects of these changes are separated from other variances. At the same time performance standards should also reflect the highest level of efficient working rather than being

based upon past achievement, it being possible that past performance was itself less than perfect.

The means of providing distribution management with feedback
on the performance of the plan must also be considered.
Distribution reporting systems have been identified as a vital part
of the logistics information system (see Chapter 6). As yet,
however, too many organisations supply their distribution managers with only rudimentary information through regular performance reports. The planning tasks described above follow a logical
sequence from the audit through to monitoring and control.
Indeed the whole process should ideally be viewed as a cycle (see
figure 9.2) whereby the distribution plan becomes a continuing
activity, guiding the direction taken and providing a firm base for
the allocation of resources.

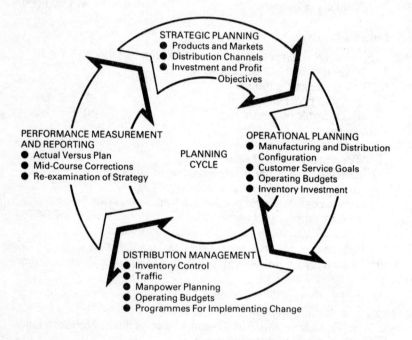

Source: Jack Moore, 'Strategic Considerations in Measuring and Reporting
          Performance for Physical Distribution Management', *NCPDM Annual Meeting
          Proceedings*, 1977.

Figure 9.2   The distribution planning cycle

Decision support systems in distribution planning

The discipline imposed upon the distribution function by the planning process has led to the search for aids to the management of this task. In recent years developments in computer-based modelling and simulation techniques have made possible the creation of so-called 'decision support systems'.

With the assistance of these systems managers can quickly compare trade-offs among a variety of strategic and operational options to identify optimum, or improved, solutions to logistics problems. In its simplest form a decision support system is a computer-based model that describes the process to be managed, e.g. the distribution system, combined with a data base which contains actual data on the operating characteristics of the system, e.g. costs, demand etc. The computer can then be instructed to answer a vast number of 'what if' type questions. For example: what if this depot were to be closed; what if inventory coverage on these items was to be reduced, what if order cycle time was to be reduced by one day. The answers would detail the effects of such changes on service levels, total system costs and other operating characteristics.

A recent study[4] on the use of decision support systems in logistics management reported some typical applications:

> Agrico chemical company, by cooperation between corporate and outside management science consultants, has implemented an integrated computer-based production, distribution and inventory management system. This system, which is used exclusively to evaluate the cost/benefit impact of alternative capital investments, has, according to Agrico management, already saved over $40 million.

> International Paper, under the direction of the corporate OR group, has developed a general purpose decision support system to help make resource allocation decisions. The scope includes operational, tactical and strategic planning from the woodlands, through all the intermediate processing, and the distribution of finished primary and byproducts. The system has identified significant cost improvement opportunities and has been quoted as having substantially reduced the level of contention surrounding resource allocation decisions.

> The R & G Sloane Manufacturing Company, a leading manufacturer of plastic pipes and fittings for the building and chemical industries, utilised a management support system to

aid in production and sales planning. The system is credited with an increase of 13 per cent in generating profits during a recent year.

Whilst it is beyond the scope of this book to discuss the technical aspects of model building and simulation in great detail it is nevertheless now becoming such an important management concern and, as the above examples demonstrate, a practical device for improving profitability, that a brief review of the field is appropriate.

Model building and simulation

A 'model' is a representation of relationships within a system. At the simplest level these may be expressed in verbal terms such as 'an increase in service levels will improve our market share'. At a more sophisticated level such relationships would be quantified and made more specific, for example 'given no change in competitive actions and general economic conditions a change from 95 per cent in-stock availability to 97 per cent on product X will result in an increase in market share from 23 to 26 per cent'. The more complex models will often consist of a number of such statements so that the model is in effect a set of interrelated quantified relationships. Models need not be designed to be 'predictive', their primary use may be for explanation. This is particularly the case where models of market behaviour are to be constructed.

Indeed there is a whole 'family' of models, and the choice of the appropriate type will depend upon the use to which it is to be put. Increasingly the emphasis is not so much on the construction of 'optimising' models, that is those which will generate a unique solution that cannot be bettered. Rather there is a recognition that the complexity of real-world relationships is such that such optima, if they exist at all, may not be attainable. Instead it is frequently more realistic to seek to identify outcomes which are the 'best currently available' or the 'best yet identified'. It is here that simulation as a technique comes into its own. Simulation is not an optimising technique, but an approach to evaluating alternative options using models of the system under consideration. In the same way a car designer would use wind tunnel tests to identify improved body designs to reduce drag, so too can the logistics planner use simulation to identify solutions which give better results than others.

One of the problems with simulation, at least until recently, has been that the construction of the model to represent the system is often a time-consuming and complex task. However there are now many widely available computer software packages which enable any organisation's logistics system to be adequately represented (see, for example,[5]). There still remains the need to generate an adequate data base using actual data from the recent past, for example: daily demand, item by item; vehicle capacity; transport costs; labour rates etc. Once this is to hand the system can be simulated using actual data (see figure 9.3) to ascertain the extent to which it reproduces actual outcome, e.g. customer service levels. This is a validation procedure necessary to ensure the accuracy of the system representation. Given that a high degree of validity is established management can now begin to use the model as a decision support system. In other words 'what if' questions can be asked and answered. This is the real power of simulation and it is one of the most important management techniques available to the distribution planner. It will probably revolutionise distribution planning and strategy formulation in the future.

Industrial dynamics

Often considerable insights can be gained into the 'dynamics' of a logistics system through the use of simulation. This is because in most logistics systems there will be 'leads and lags', in other words the response to an input or a change in the system may be delayed. For example the presence of a warehouse or a stockholding intermediary in the distribution channel can cause a substantial distortion in demand at the factory. This is due to the 'acceleration effect' which can cause self-generated fluctuations in the operating characteristics of a system.

Taking the example of a manufacturing company that sells its output to a wholesaler, who then sells it to retailers, it is possible to illustrate the effect of accelerated relationships. The company has a service policy which requires it to keep the equivalent of eight weeks' stock as a buffer; the wholesaler keeps twelve weeks' stock and the retailer three weeks' stock. For some reason, say a promotion, final consumer demand increases in the month by 10 per cent over the previous month. If the retailer wishes to maintain his previous service level he will increase his order to the wholesaler not by 10 but by 11 per cent (i.e. $10 + 10 \, (3/52)$) in order to maintain three weeks' safety stock. The wholesaler is now faced with an increase in demand of 11 per cent which, if he

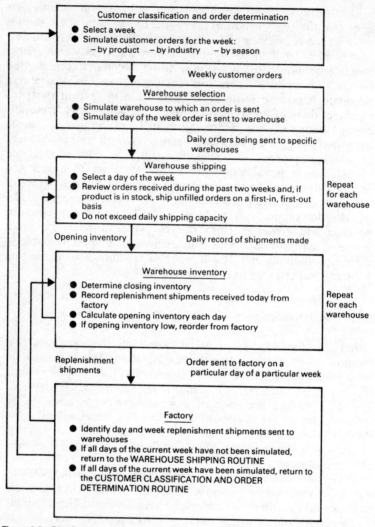

Figure 9.3   Distribution system simulation

readjusts his stock levels, will result in an increase in his monthly order to the manufacturer of 13 per cent (i.e. 11 + 11 (12/52)). Similarly, the manufacturer producing for stock and wishing to maintain eight weeks' safety stock increases production by 15 per cent (i.e. 13 + 13 (8/52)). Thus an initial increase in consumer demand of 10 per cent has resulted in an eventual increase in production of 15 per cent. If final demand were to fall back in the next period the same process in reverse would be experienced.

Taking concepts such as the acceleration effect and the interrelationships within complex business systems Forrester has developed the notion of 'industrial dynamics'[6] which he defined as:

> The study of the information feedback characteristics of industrial activity to show how organisational structure, amplification (in policies) and time delays (in decisions and returns) interact to influence the success of the enterprise. It treats the interactions between the flows of information, money, orders, materials, personnel, and capital equipment in a company, an industry, or a national economy.
>
> Industrial dynamics provides a single framework for integrating the functional areas of management – marketing, production, accounting, research and development, and capital investment.

Using a specially developed computer simulation language, DYNAMO, Forrester built a model of a production-distribution system involving three levels in the distribution channel: a retailer's inventory, a distributor's inventory, and a factory inventory. Each level was interconnected through information flows and flows of goods. The model used real-world relationships and data and included parameters such as order transmission times, order processing times, factory lead times and shipment delivery times. Management could then examine the effects on the total system of, say, a change in retail sales or the impact of changing production patterns or any other policy change or combination of changes.

If the industrial dynamics logic is applied to the earlier example of the manufacturer-wholesaler-retailer stock adjustment effect, the disturbance that is caused throughout the system with the resultant effect on service levels is shown in figure 9.4.

Using simulation in this way can thus help to explain the reasons for fluctuations in a system as well as providing a guide to management action to overcome these effects.[7]

Demand management and the distribution plan

A new area of management concern has recently arisen, partly through the discipline brought about by the use of DRP, which has come to be termed 'demand management'.

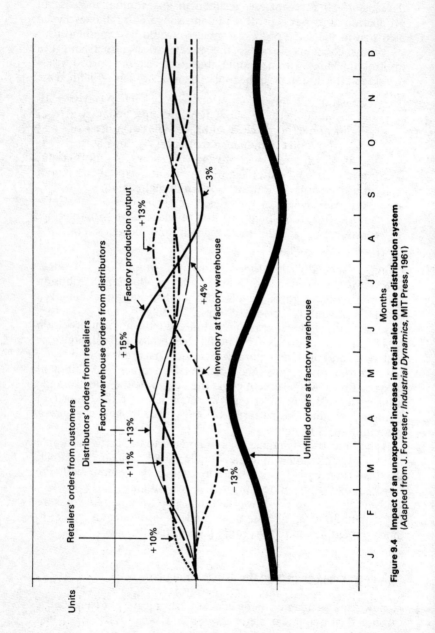

Figure 9.4   Impact of an unexpected increase in retail sales on the distribution system (Adapted from J. Forrester, *Industrial Dynamics*, MIT Press, 1961)

Units

Retailers' orders from customers

Distributors' orders from retailers

Factory warehouse orders from distributors

Factory production output
+13%

+15%

+11%   +13%

+10%

Inventory at factory warehouse
+4%

−13%

−3%

Unfilled orders at factory warehouse

Months

J   F   M   A   M   J   J   A   S   O   N   D

The concept of demand management is a combination of the sales forecasting tasks, order processing and sales management. Whilst the sales forecast anticipates demand and the order processing system enters that demand, sales management takes decisions, where necessary, relating to that demand, e.g. product substitution, product upgrade, order rotation, partial shipment, split shipment, or back ordering. Thus demand management 'generates information on sales forecasts by item, customer satisfaction, demand versus shipment, capacity versus demand, and deployment of existing inventory'.[8] Figure 9.5 shows the relationship of this view of demand management to the planning task.

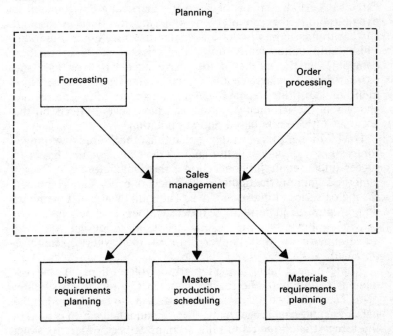

Planning

Figure 9.5 Demand management

As noted in Chapter 7, the only items to be forecast are those where demand is independent; the demand for all other items is calculated. One of the problems is that the number of stock keeping units (SKUs) that need to be forecast as independent demand items can often be very high, particularly as DRP requires separate forecasts from each stock location. DRP also requires time-phased forecasts so seasonality, cyclicality etc. must be incorporated.

There are many forecasting techniques available, some simple, many highly complicated.[9] However, for the short-term forecasting of SKU demand it is really only 'statistical' methods that will be appropriate. These techniques are based on the 'statistical projection of the past into the future' to quote one of the leading exponents of these methods, R. G. Brown.[10] Whilst there may be no alternative to using past sales data to forecast the future, this approach should be used with care.

One source of potential error in such forecasts is the assumption that what happened in the past will be repeated in the future and that trends and patterns presently discernible will continue. Often such an approach is acceptable for the short term, but not for extended periods. This is because the marketing environment is dynamic and factors can intervene to negate the effects of past and current trends, e.g. an overseas competitor may enter a market. This would quite clearly upset the sales forecasts of existing companies in the market if they have been based on past and current data. Similarly changes in consumer tastes, the development of substitute technologies, government intervention and changes in the national economy can have severe effects on the accuracy of forecasts based on extrapolation.

Thus for longer-term strategic planning other, more qualitative, forecasts may provide a better guide. One technique that has been successfully used in this connection is the 'Delphi forecast'. This is a method whereby the opinions of a panel of experts are combined through a series of questionnaires. The individual panel members do not know the identity of the other members to avoid bias and to provide anonymity. The results are used to design the next questionnaire so that convergence of the expert opinion is obtained.

Whatever techniques are adopted the role of demand management is to integrate the resulting forecasts into the distribution plan. This will often mean that forecasts need to be adjusted in the light of managerial judgements; that demand data which is used in the forecast is corrected to take account of back orders, product substitutions etc.; and that the effects of system dynamics can be factored into the final forecast. Therefore demand management can be seen as a crucial component of the distribution planning task, mediating between data, statistical technique, customer contact and the order processing system.

Attention paid to improving demand management can have substantial rewards, in the words of one writer:[11]

How many companies could benefit from a system where marketing was selling the same thing that manufacturing was making, that inventory was replenishing, that finance was budgeting and that customer service was promising?

* * * * * * *

Decision support systems in action

The lack of relevant data was one of the reasons why the Shaklee Corporation in the USA decided to install a management support system. 'We convinced (top) management that the condition of our data base was so poor that we ran the risk of making lousy decisions,' says Charles D. Fry, manager of materials analysis and planning. At the same time, the Emeryville (Calif.) producer of food supplements, cosmetics, and household cleaners was growing so fast – from $10 million in annual sales 10 years ago to $350 million in 1979 – that management was making decisions on a subjective and political basis, he says.

To build its data base, Shaklee has fed in data on plant locations, products made, cost per unit, and production capacity for its three facilities and 20 contract manufacturers. It also has stored details on more than 500 line items, 360 customers, and its 100 distribution centers. The first task was finding the best way to reduce delivery times to customers without increasing production or distribution costs. The system calculated the impact that various delivery requirements would have on transportation costs, the cost of operating distribution centers, and the cost of carrying inventories.

'For the first time,' Fry says, 'management is able to understand the financial impact associated with various service-level decisions.' Without the computer model, he says, 'there is no quantifiable way to determine the cost. And decisions become political issues between the sales side of the company, which would like a warehouse in any town where there is a reasonable demand, and the distribution side, which wants to minimize costs.'

Besides finding a way to speed up deliveries to customers and save money, too, Shaklee believes that setting up the new system forced the company to develop its comprehensive data base, which it can use to analyze other operating problems. But it was a big step. All told, it took six months and $250,000 to develop the data base and model. It can often take up to two years to get such a system running. And annual maintenance costs run to about 20% of the initial expenditure.

Business Week, 21 Jan, 1980

Notes

1   R. E. Murray, 'Strategic Distribution Planning: Structuring the Plan' in *Proceedings of the Eighteenth Annual Conference of the National Council of Physical Distribution Management*, Chicago, October 1980.

2   J. Heskett *et al.*, *Business Logistics*, Ronald Press, 1973.

3   R. Ballou, *Business Logistics Management*, Prentice Hall, 1973.

4   D. J. Closs and O. K. Helferich, 'Logistics Decision Support System: An Integration of Information, Data Base and Modeling Systems to Aid the Logistics Practitioner' in *Journal of Business Logistics*, vol. 3, no. 2, 1982.

5   A. Waller, 'Computer Systems for Distribution Planning', *International Journal of Physical Distribution and Materials Management*, vol. 13, no. 7, 1984.

6   J. W. Forrester, *Industrial Dynamics*, MIT Press, 1961.

7   R. G. Coyle, *Management System Dynamics*, John Wiley & Sons, 1977.

8   J. W. Muir, 'Manufacturing Resource Planning and Demand Management' in *Components of Manufacturing Resource Planning*, Auerbach Publishers Inc., 1981.

9   S. C. Wheelwright and S. Makridakis, *Forecasting Methods for Management*, 3rd ed., Wiley Interscience, 1980.

10 R. G. Brown, *Statistical Forecasting for Inventory Control*, McGraw-Hill, 1959.

11 J. W. Muir and T. L. Newberry, 'Management's Role in a Forecasting System' in *American Production & Inventory Control Society 24th Annual Conference Proceedings*, Boston, USA, 1981.

10 Implementing logistics strategy

It is probably the case that many companies now understand the 'total distribution concept' and the need for a logistics orientation in managing the flow of materials and goods through their business and marketing channels. Whilst this recognition is by no means universal, it might be justified to claim that at least the level of awareness of the importance of 'thinking logistically' is higher than ever before. The problem is how to move beyond awareness to implementation.

Many managers have no problem in accepting the concept of total distribution, but encounter severe difficulties in making it work within the organisation. This is due partly to the fact that new skills are called for in the management of the total logistics activity, partly to a lack of top management commitment and partly to organisational barriers.

The basic skills

What are these skills that are essential to the efficient management of the logistics task within the firm? Firstly, as noted several times in this book, logistics management is a total systems concept with a span of concern which ultimately encompasses all the movement and storage activities within the firm and its distribution channels. This means that those called upon to manage the activity must understand the total business and take a broader view of the impact of decisions made in one area which are likely to have systems-wide effects.

Secondly, logistics is ultimately concerned with customer service and specifically with making the product available in the marketplace within defined cost and service parameters. This implies a concern for the marketing impact of logistics systems. In many companies there is a general neglect of distribution as a component in the marketing mix. The notion of the 'four Ps' – product, price, promotion and place – tends in reality to be concerned with the first three whilst the fourth, place, is not viewed as a strategic marketing variable.

Thirdly, a major requirement for developing effective logistics management is the need for a close liaison with the operations management of the business. The link between supply, production and distribution is vital. Indeed the importance of these interface areas is heightened by the use of requirements planning techniques.

Thus ideally the logistics manager requires a high level of skills in business analysis, marketing strategy and systems management in addition to those necessary to the day-to-day running of a distribution network.

The need for commitment

Beyond the skills of the logistics management team lies a vital prerequisite for success in implementing logistics strategy. Nothing will happen in an organisation which lacks the commitment of top management to the logistics concept and the will to reshape, where necessary, the organisation structure.

Because the logistics concept cuts directly across established functional boundaries and 'territories' in the business many people need to be persuaded of the need to change the way they do things. Change of this sort is unlikely to be implemented without direction from the top. Suboptimisation through individual functions operating without regard for the wider system is common in those organisations where the chief executive officer does not understand the logistics concept. Even strong enthusiasm from the distribution manager cannot overcome alone the entrenched working practices in a conventionally managed business. It is interesting to note that companies often regarded as leaders in the development of logistics-oriented organisations are those where there is the highest level of commitment to the concept. In Europe companies like Philips, Rank Xerox, Volvo and Kelloggs have achieved substantial success in implementing logistics strategies because of a high level of commitment from the top down.

Organisational barriers

It has long been recognised that one of the strongest barriers to change within a firm is the organisation structure itself. There is always a tendency towards ossification within any organisational format, i.e. the longer systems and procedures have been established the harder they are to change.

Beyond this natural inertia there lies a bigger problem of intra-organisational conflict brought aboout by the differing objectives pursued by different functional areas. Thus, for example, the production schedules adopted by the operations manager may not lead to an optimal inventory position from the distribution manager's point of view. Similarly, the desire by the distribution manager to consolidate outbound shipments might not meet the customer service objectives sought by the marketing function.

Such conflicts arise not only through differences between the goals of the various functions concerned but also through different perceptions of what is important. The view of the world is heavily influenced by the place in which one stands and this is nowhere more true than within a business organisation. It is only through improved communication and the development of superordinate goals that organisational barriers to change can be removed and hence the implementation of logistics strategies be made possible. With this in mind the remainder of this chapter is devoted to a discussion of alternative approaches to developing appropriate organisational structures for logistics management.

The organisational task

Writing about organisations in general Lawrence and Lorsch[1] developed a 'contingency' model which recognised the need for the organisational structure of the firm to reflect the nature of the environment in which it operated. In this regard, they emphasised the earlier findings of Chandler[2] who had shown how the structure of organisations follows from, and is guided by, strategic decisions. A further conclusion highlighted by Chandler was that 'wherever the executives responsible for the firm fail to create offices and structure necessary to bring together effectively the several administrative offices into a unified whole, they fail to carry out one of their basic economic roles'.[3]

Developing this argument Lawrence and Lorsch designed the twin concepts of 'differentiation' and 'integration', both of which have implications for logistics organisation. Differentiation is defined as 'the difference in cognitive and emotional orientation among managers in different functional departments'. Integration is defined as 'the quality of the state of collaboration that exists among departments that are required to achieve unity of effort by the demands of the environment'. These twin concepts are particularly relevant in the context of logistics management. Firstly, as we have seen, the fragmentation of logistics tasks in many organisations leads to substantial 'differentiation' between functions. At the same time because of the interrelations between these tasks the need for 'integration' is high.

Building upon these ideas Persson[4] has suggested a 'contingency' approach to logistics organisation. Based upon a study of Scandinavian companies Persson demonstrates that there is a tendency in organisations to develop different organisation design strategies for logistics coordination in a specific pattern. Three factors seem to explain this pattern; logistics task predictability; the number of logistics decision elements, and the extent to which logistics activities can be made into an autonomous function.

Logistics task predictability is indicated by the extent to which the firm produces to stock. Task predictability will be higher the more the firm produces to stock.

The number of decision elements is indicated by the size of the organisation, the number of products and the complexity of the products measured in terms of their components. Thus the number of logistics decision elements is high when the organisation is relatively large, when the range of products is wide and/or the products are complex in their nature.

Where clearly separate product groups exist in terms of technology, markets or location then a high degree of potential *logistics decision autonomy* will exist.

Using this framework Persson suggested that the lower the task predictability the greater would be the need for informal rules and procedures, but that with greater predictability the use of formal systems and procedures would increase. In situations characterised by few decision elements then a functional organisation of the traditional type would be adequate. However as the number of decision elements increased the greater would be the need for a flow-oriented organisation structure. Finally the degree of autonomy would influence the extent to which distribution might appropriately be centralised or decentralised. This is an issue to which we shall return later.

There are some similarities between the first two of the three elements (task predictability and number of decision elements) with the two-dimensional matrix proposed by Hayes and Wheelwright[5] in the analysis of manufacturing strategies. This approach looked at the combined effects of product structure and process structure. As figure 10.1 illustrates, different product/process combinations might require alternative means of managing the logistics tasks within those organisations.

It can be inferred from this matrix that the approach to logistics organisation will differ according to the particular product/process characteristics of the business in question. Managing logistics in a sugar refinery is obviously a different task from that encountered in a commercial printers, for example.

What can be discerned from these various models is that whilst the need for logistical coordination is always present, the extent to which it affects the organisation structure of the firm can differ greatly. As shown in Chapter 1, logistics is first and foremost a planning framework and a means of achieving coordination in the chain of materials flow. What therefore is required organisationally is not necessarily a 'logistics function' but an organisation structure that is appropriate to the contingencies of product, process and task.

From the framework presented in figure 10.1 it can be seen that the need for formalised, flow-oriented organisational structures becomes more necessary the closer the business is to the bottom right hand corner of the matrix. At the top left hand corner, on the other hand, the need is for flexible scheduling, for control of work in progress and delivery lead-times and the requirement for formal logistics organisation structures is reduced.

Considering those industrial situations or 'contingencies' which tend towards the bottom right corner of the product/process matrix, it is suggested that the need is for an organisational approach that could best be described as 'flow-oriented'.

Flow-oriented logistics systems

Logistics, as observed many times in this book, is concerned with the management of materials flow and the related information flow from the point of entry to the system through to the final sale. In the larger organisations different products will be manufactured and marketed to different customer groups. Similarly many component parts or raw materials may be involved in the manufacture or assembly of the products, involving multiple points of contacts with suppliers. It makes great sense therefore to

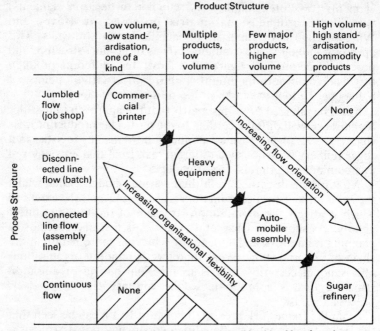

Source: Based on R. H. Hayes and S. L. Wheelwright, 'Matching Manufacturing
           Process and Product Life Cycles' in *Harvard Business Review*, Jan.-Feb., 1979.

Figure 10.1   Product/process structure

seek to develop management and control systems which mirror
this materials flow.

The basic problem to be tackled in the traditionally-organised
company is that functions are managed rather than flows. Such an
organisation will have a built-in tendency to optimise functional
performance with the consequent possibility of reducing the ability
of the organisation as a whole to service its customers most
cost-effectively. Some commentators have suggested that it may
be possible to overcome this problem by introducing a form of
matrix management.[6]

The concept of matrix management has emerged from its early
beginnings at NASA, where it was developed in response to the
need to coordinate the complex space programme which involved
over 20,000 industrial contractors, subcontractors and supplier
organisations. Here the emphasis was very much upon managing
the programme or mission, since in effect there were a limited

number of objectives that NASA wished to achieve in a fixed time frame.

It may be possible to envisage such an extreme form of organisation in which the overriding authority resides in the programmes with the functions providing inputs as required. However such an approach is just as likely to be suboptimal as the functional organisation, this time because of potential overlap and duplication of resources between programmes and the lack of a total systems viewpoint.

The version of matrix management that has evolved from this idea recognises the importance of both the inputs (the functions) and the outputs (the programmes or missions). It does not make particular sense to focus upon one at the expense of the other. Instead matrix management, as it is practised in mány organisations around the world, is essentially a 'shared authority' system with the objective of achieving a balance between the needs of functions and programmes.[7] Because logistics is essentially a customer-focused activity involving the coordination of inputs from functional areas such as marketing, production and transport, the matrix management concept may be a particularly appropriate organisational model.

One of the biggest problems with the matrix concept in practice is that it presumes an ideal world where programme managers, e.g. logistics managers, and functional managers, e.g. marketing managers, are prepared to share authority and to work together for the greater good of the organisation.[8] In reality this is often not the case and conflict can occur. Frustrations are encountered by those who work at the 'interstices' of the matrix, i.e. the points of contact between functions and programmes. It is not always easy to work in a situation where in effect there are 'two bosses'.

Nevertheless in many situations the matrix organisation makes sense as a means of managing materials flow in the most cost-effective way. Ultimately the ability to make the matrix work in a logistics management context will depend upon the clear identification of customer-focused goals and a high degree of task definition at both the functional and the programme level. Table 10.1 provides an indication of the type of task differentiation between functional and programme responsibilities.

It is unlikely that a functionally organised company would introduce major organisational change in order to enable effective logistics management to be achieved. Indeed such change may not always be necessary; a lot will depend upon the firm's position on the product/process matrix discussed earlier. However, for those companies where flow-oriented management makes particular

Table 10.1
Programme and functional managers' responsibilities

Programme manager	*Functional manager*
Programme direction	*Operational direction*
Directs corporate programmes and coordinates functional inputs to achieve programme objectives	Determines who will perform detailed tasks, where they will be done and how they will be accomplished
Develops programme plans	Provides a stable base for the development of talent and skills to assure maintenance of technical capability
Determines and issues the work breakdown, structure and related work statements, budgets, and schedules which define what effort will be accomplished, when it will be performed, and who will have accountability.	Provides necessary facilities and services to support programme requirements
Assures the attainment of the output and cost objectives of the programme within schedule	*Operational control*
	Responsible for the technical excellence and quality requirements of assigned tasks
Programme control	Assures that all tasks are accomplished within technical specifications, on schedule and within budget.
Monitoring cost, schedule and technical results against master programme plans	
Replans and rebudgets as necessary to assure accomplishment of programme objectives	*Administration*
Monitoring contractual reporting	Performs administrative services in support of personnel assigned to a programme.
	Initiates merit increases for all personnel within his function.
Customer coordination	
Provides the prime contact with the customer for programme activities	
Administration	
Approves the assignment of key functional personnel assigned to the programme	

Source: Based upon R. E. Shannon, 'Matrix Management Structures' in *Industrial Engineering*, March 1972.

Table 10.1
nctional managers' responsibilities

Functional manager

Operational direction

Determines who will perform detailed tasks, where they will be done and how they will be accomplished

Provides a stable base for the development of talent and skills to assure maintenance of technical capability

Provides necessary facilities and services to support programme requirements

Operational control

Responsible for the technical excellence and quality requirements of assigned tasks

Assures that all tasks are accomplished within technical specifications, on schedule and within budget.

Administration

Performs administrative services in support of personnel assigned to a programme.

Initiates merit increases for all personnel within his function.

hannon, 'Matrix Management
ing, March 1972.

elements (task predictability and number of decision elements) with the two-dimensional matrix proposed by Hayes and Wheelwright[5] in the analysis of manufacturing strategies. This approach looked at the combined effects of product structure and process structure. As figure 10.1 illustrates, different product/process combinations might require alternative means of managing the logistics tasks within those organisations.

It can be inferred from this matrix that the approach to logistics organisation will differ according to the particular product/process characteristics of the business in question. Managing logistics in a sugar refinery is obviously a different task from that encountered in a commercial printers, for example.

What can be discerned from these various models is that whilst the need for logistical coordination is always present, the extent to which it affects the organisation structure of the firm can differ greatly. As shown in Chapter 1, logistics is first and foremost a planning framework and a means of achieving coordination in the chain of materials flow. What therefore is required organisationally is not necessarily a 'logistics function' but an organisation structure that is appropriate to the contingencies of product, process and task.

From the framework presented in figure 10.1 it can be seen that the need for formalised, flow-oriented organisational structures becomes more necessary the closer the business is to the bottom right hand corner of the matrix. At the top left hand corner, on the other hand, the need is for flexible scheduling, for control of work in progress and delivery lead-times and the requirement for formal logistics organisation structures is reduced.

Considering those industrial situations or 'contingencies' which tend towards the bottom right corner of the product/process matrix, it is suggested that the need is for an organisational approach that could best be described as 'flow-oriented'.

Flow-oriented logistics systems

Logistics, as observed many times in this book, is concerned with the management of materials flow and the related information flow from the point of entry to the system through to the final sale. In the larger organisations different products will be manufactured and marketed to different customer groups. Similarly many component parts or raw materials may be involved in the manufacture or assembly of the products, involving multiple points of contacts with suppliers. It makes great sense therefore to

Product Structure

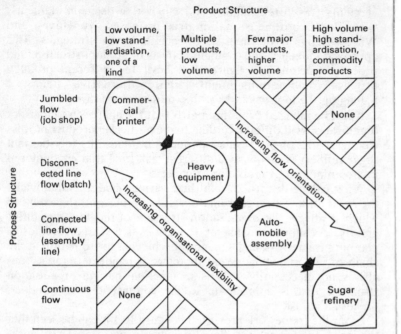

Source: Based on R. H. Hayes and S. L. Wheelwright, 'Matching Manufacturing
           Process and Product Life Cycles' in *Harvard Business Review*, Jan.-Feb., 1979.

Figure 10.1   Product/process structure

seek to develop management and control systems which mirror
this materials flow.

The basic problem to be tackled in the traditionally-organised
company is that functions are managed rather than flows. Such an
organisation will have a built-in tendency to optimise functional
performance with the consequent possibility of reducing the ability
of the organisation as a whole to service its customers most
cost-effectively. Some commentators have suggested that it may
be possible to overcome this problem by introducing a form of
matrix management.[6]

The concept of matrix management has emerged from its early
beginnings at NASA, where it was developed in response to the
need to coordinate the complex space programme which involved
over 20,000 industrial contractors, subcontractors and supplie
organisations. Here the emphasis was very much upon managing
the programme or mission, since in effect there were a limited

Programme and fu

Programme manager

Programme direction

Directs corporate progra
and coordinates functi
inputs to achieve progra
objectives

Develops programme plan

Determines and issues the
breakdown, structure and
lated work statements, budg
and schedules which de
what effort will be acc
plished, when it will be
formed, and who will h
accountability.

Assures the attainment of
output and cost objectives
the programme within sched

Programme control

Monitoring cost, schedule a
technical results against mast
programme plans

Replans and rebudgets
necessary to assure accomplish
ment of programme objective

Monitoring   contractua
reporting

Customer coordination

Provides the prime contact with
the customer for programme
activities

Administration

Approves the assignment of
key functional personnel
assigned to the programme

Source: Based upon R. E. S
Structures' in *Industrial Enginee*

sense it is often possible to achieve partial logistics integration without recourse to matrix management. One such means is based upon the management of 'work flow'.[9]

The approach begins with the flow-charting of work activities within the logistics function in the sequence in which they occur. For example, consider the order processing system where orders enter the system, are processed, inventory is allocated, orders are assembled and shipped – all accompanied by paper flow and documentation of one type or another. In many companies different functions may have an involvement in the total order processing system. Sales administration may handle order entry and order acknowledgement, the accounts department may be responsible for credit control, the production department may be responsible for stock control and distribution looks after the warehouse and traffic! Such a situation is not unusual and can lead to many inefficiencies. A work-flow solution would be to bring these related tasks together under the unified control of one person who would supervise the management of the entire process, working within guidelines and policies determined by sales, accounting and distribution etc. – in other words a separation of policy, e.g. credit control and service levels, from execution.

One of the biggest stimuli to the adoption of the work-flow management concept in logistics has been the computer. Its growing use for order entry, order processing, stock allocation, documentation etc. has often forced companies to reorganise around the work flow since that is precisely the focus for the computer in its logical, step-by-step, approach to management tasks.

Autonomy in logistics

One further variable to contend with in the implementation of logistics strategy is the extent to which organisational autonomy is desirable for the logistics activity in the firm.

This issue can crop up in a variety of forms. For example, should logistics be a function in its own right? Should logistics be represented at board level in its own right? Should logistics be centralised or decentralised? Can logistics be spun off as a separate profit centre? Of course there is no one answer to these questions as it will depend entirely on the specific situation. However, there are some principles which can guide the firm in its decision on where to position the logistics task organisationally.

As far as the question of a separate logistics function is concerned, this is only really appropriate in a flow-process type business, for example an oil refinery; the reason being that in a sense logistics is the business in this context. The same argument can be made in relation to the necessity for board level representation.

Closely connected with this is the question of whether logistics should be centralised or decentralised. In some cases a strong case may be made for the centralisation of some functions, e.g. purchasing, and the decentralisation of others, e.g. warehousing. From a purely logistical point of view the greater the degree of centralisation the better from the point of coordination and integration of activities. Similarly the centralisation of such activities as transport, warehousing, order processing etc. will permit greater economies of scale. However, from a marketing and even a production point of view the opposite may be the case. Ultimately the extent of diversity amongst products and served markets should determine the degree of decentralisation necessary. If the firm itself operates on a decentralised basis, say product divisions, then there may also be a case for decentralisation in logistics, perhaps with some degree of central coordination on a staff basis.

The answer to the question of logistical autonomy and degree of decentralisation is sometimes provided by establishing the logistics function as a profit centre. Under this mode of management the logistics activity, or as many parts of it that could sensibly be put together, would be separately managed as a financial entity. It is usually suggested that to be truly a profit centre an activity must (a) employ capital; (b) incur costs; (c) add value, and (d) set price.

There can be no question about the first three; logistics clearly employs capital, incurs cost and adds value. As far as price is concerned there is no reason why a separately constituted logistics entity could not charge its customers for its services on a transfer charge basis. The attractiveness of the profit centre option is increasing as more companies explore the possibilities. Many companies now operate their transport and warehousing function on this basis and some have even extended the profit centre concept to include materials management.[10]

In a decentralised company operating on a divisional basis the logistics profit centre may provide a means of achieving economies of scale whilst still tailoring its services to meet the needs of its 'clients' – the divisions. In those companies that have followed this route and where there is freedom of action by both the divisions and the logistics profit centre – that is, to do business with each other or not depending upon the cost/benefits – higher efficiency and profitability are reported.

Getting started

Whilst for many the objective is clear, the distance from the present position to the goal may seem daunting. It may make more sense to be content with incremental change albeit with the ultimate intention of achieving those far off goals. This is particularly true in the process of implementing logistics strategy, particularly when the starting point may be an organisation with only a rudimentary, fragmented system for managing the materials flow.

Some interesting findings that confirm this view emerged from a recent study from A. T. Kearney & Co.[11] They looked at twenty-seven companies that had successfully implemented logistics productivity improvement programmes and found that a number of common characteristics emerged:

> They *manage the process of change* with the same attention as the management of day-to-day operations.
>
> They tend to *employ a project orientation* for change with clear objective setting and, in most companies, measurement of the results achieved.
>
> They tend to *focus on real productivity* gains from improved utilisation and performance and from change of operational technology, rather than simply 'cost reduction'. This tends to require physical rather than financial measurement systems.
>
> They *achieved early success*, perhaps modest, and built more ambitious programmes as they gained experience and support. Conversely, most programmes that failed were a result of 'biting off more than they could chew' too early in the process.
>
> They have a *good communications* programme upward, laterally, and downward which publicises success and shares the credit.
>
> In virtually every really successful programme, there is a single *key executive* considered its motivating force by peers and the company.

The same survey also pointed out that successful implementation of logistics productivity improvement programmes tended to come from the piecemeal, or step by step, approach rather than from a holistic 'grand slam'. Thus strategies that have a more limited focus, such as improving vehicle utilisation or integrating order processing with inventory replenishment or warehouse rationalisation, are more likely to lead to the achievement of improvement in overall logistics improvement.

Thinking big but moving slowly is possibly the best rule in implementing strategies in an area as complex as logistics. Whilst the rate of progress may be frustrating the ultimate rewards will be substantial.

Notes

1   P. R. Lawrence and J. W. Lorsch, *Organization and Environment*, Harvard University Press, 1967.
2   A. Chandler, *Strategy and Structure: Chapters in the History of Industrial Enterprise*, MIT Press, Cambridge, 1963.
3   Ibid., p. 16.
4   G. Persson, 'Organisation Design Strategies for Business Logistics' in *International Journal of Physical Distribution and Materials Management*, vol. 8, no. 6, 1978.
5   R. A. Hayes and S. C. Wheelwright, 'Matching Manufacturing Process and Product Life Cycles' in *Harvard Business Review*, January-February 1979.
6   D. W. De Hayes and R. L. Taylor, 'Making Logistics Work in a Firm' in *Business Horizons*, June 1972.
7   S. M. Davis and P. R. Lawrence, *Matrix*, Addison-Wesley, 1977.
8   De Hayes and Taylor, 'Matrix Management and Logistics', op. cit.
9   E. O. Chapple and L. R. Sayles, *The Measure of Management*, Macmillan, 1961, pp. 19-45.
10 D. S. Ammer, 'Materials Management as a Profit Center' in *Harvard Business Review*, January-February 1969.
11 J. E. Morehouse, W. J. Best and W. J. Markham, 'Improving Logistics Productivity: The Successful Companies' in *NCPDM Annual Conference Proceedings*, 1983.

Index